WEIRD CHURCH

WELCOME TO THE
TWENTY-FIRST CENTURY

Beth Ann Estock and Paul Nixon

THE PILGRIM PRESS

CLEVELAND

DEDICATION

In gratitude for the communion of saints from ancient times until present—in particular our parents, Joy and Joe Estock and Larry and Sonia Nixon—who brought us up in the traditional church surrounded by love and nurtured in the stories of faith.

In hope for the saints of the future— our children, Hannah Joy Petrillo, Sarah Rose Petrillo, and Jonathan Nixon, and whatever children and grandchildren they may have— that they will find their dance with the Triune God in weird and wonderful ways!

The Pilgrim Press, 700 Prospect Avenue, Cleveland, Ohio 44115
thepilgrimpress.com
© 2016 by Beth Ann Estock and Paul Nixon

Printed in the United States of America on acid-free paper

19   18   17   16   15   5   4   3   2   1

ISBN 978-0-8298-2034-8

CONTENTS

INITIUM

The Colors of Cultural Revolution

There is a Catholic church just outside the tourist gates of the Forum in Rome called Santa Francesca Romana. It is built on the ruins of the Temple of Venus and Rome. According to legend, this church sits on the place in which Simon Magus wanted to prove his powers as stronger than those of the apostles and started levitating in front of Peter and Paul. The two apostles fell on their knees preaching, and Simon fell, dying. This church is just steps away from the Arch of Constantine that marks one of the greatest turning points in history—the military coup that eventually made Christianity the mainstream religion of the empire, about seventeen hundred years ago.

On a summer day in 2014 in a sea of tourists, the bells chimed for the 11 AM Sunday Mass. Curiously Beth walked in to find that the priest was the only person in the sanctuary. The ancient space was awe-inspiring and no one was there for Mass. At the epicenter of the birth of Western civilization and Christendom, no one was attending Mass. Much could be written on the reasons why that particular church is today a museum to the glorious past. But is it also a canary in the coal mine? Especially as we look toward midcentury in the United States, why do we believe that the United States will continue to be exceptional in resisting the tide of secularization that has taken Christianity in Europe to ruin?

American Christianity, as a compelling social institution, has outlived European Christianity by about half a century. We were more innovative, for one thing. And without a state church, we have typically had more church options per community than is true anywhere in Europe. Plus, for a variety of reasons, which we will address later, the social assumptions that undergirded Christendom simply lasted a bit longer on this side of the Atlantic. But, since the turn of the twenty-first century, if you have been paying any attention at all to the news about American religion, you are aware that we are becoming more like the Europeans every day. We are experiencing a vast and unprecedented exodus of Americans from organized religion, similar to what Europe saw in the years just after World War II. For every ten that leave the old-line churches, two or three stop in at the nondenominational church. And a steady trickle of frustrated young evangelicals keep traveling against the traffic back towards the liturgy, the architecture, and the more liberal possibilities of a few old churches. But the overall trajectory is grim, if you have any investment in "church-as-we-have-known-it."

"Please God, not on my watch," bishops and other denominational leaders pray under their breath, as hundreds of congregations go from full-time pastorates to less-than-full-time and then to closure and the selling of property. About a decade ago, Paul Nixon wrote a book with a bold title: *I Refuse to Lead a Dying Church*. In fact, we continue to see amazing possibilities for any church that is willing to do a deep rethink of mission and ministry and to follow the Spirit to new places, *and* which is fortunate enough to have a pastoral leader of somewhat exceptional gifting. What this means is that for every church that manages a comeback, nine do not. And even where there is a comeback this year, there is a good chance of a renewed and intensified decline in the same place just a decade or so into the future. It is truly a perilous time for institutional Christianity in America.

A few years ago, the bishops of The United Methodist Church decided (albeit briefly) that new church starts might save the denomination, since new churches have a track record of reaching new people faster than existing congregations. But over the last two decades, planting churches has become harder, and the size of the new churches launched has steadily declined. In many neighborhoods, a church planter can do everything she was supposed to do a generation ago to get two hundred people, and today she will be lucky to gather about a third of that—not enough to pay the bills. According to a recent study by Lifeway Research, the median worship attendance in an American new church start in the first year is thirty and slowly grows to seventy-two by year four. Under conventional assumptions of church with the full-time pastor-employee, the building, and the ability to send financial support to the denomination, most of our new churches are not financially viable after five years. Even with less-than-full-time pastoral leadership in many cases, nearly one-third of current American church plants will never discover financial self-sufficiency. Hence many end up failing, especially if they are dependent upon denominational money to stay alive.[1]

Once upon a time in the American heartland, circuit riders and camp meeting alumni planted churches faster than they could start the towns and cities. Today one of the Methodist bishops in the heartland longs to plant "bread and butter churches," which would grow to sufficient financial strength to build a building, pay a preacher, and send some money to headquarters. We feel his pain. With very talented and well-coached church-planting leaders here and there, we will still see more of these in the years ahead. But we will not see enough to turn the tide of the overall decline. The whole paradigm of church that has traditionally undergirded such projects is dying, along with the market of people who respond to such opportunities.

The buzzword du jour is *sustainability*. If only we can find enough money to keep these places open, maybe then the lack of people will not be so much a threat. Sustainability is important. Our company works to help churches create sustainable ministry models and to raise funds. But we do not believe that sustainability is the critical issue. Where there is spiritual vitality, the church can always find a way for sustainability. In fact, our vision would be a church that is both spiritually robust *and* able to cover its costs. The word for that would be *resilient*: a faith community that moves beyond mere financial sustainability—and that is suited for a viral replication.

No other church is as loaded financially as the Roman Catholic Church. They have the cash flow to stay in the game longer than any of us, albeit in a downsized form. Yet that image of being the only one who shows up for worship lingers in the background, twisting us in pangs of anxiety and a sense of hopelessness as if all of Christianity is falling off a cliff. We might wonder, what is the point of the priest in the empty church with his salary endowed overseeing an institution where the spiritual movement that it existed to support has died? We believe God desires something much more of the church than financial sustainability.

In the years ahead, we will see many Christian clergy just giving up on the whole enterprise of "church-as-we-have-known-it," and finding different work. Others will narrow their focus to be chaplains to an aging remnant. Still others will obsess over liturgy and pageant. More than a few will gallantly seek to organize for social justice. Some of the most highly motivated will resolve simply to try harder at the things they know how to do, with some smart tweaks, as they seek to compete for the dwindling remnant of people willing to engage. A small minority will be fortunate enough to preside over growing congregations, and many of those congregations will in fact grow to be very large, with multiple locations. But the latter will be very much the exception, and not the norm.

The Christendom world we knew is gone.

If you cannot accept yet that it's over—if you choose to dwell a few days or few years longer in the unreality that the institutional "church-as-we-have-known-it" still has significant control over the future of the Jesus movement—then you might as well stop reading right here. We can't help you with denial.

But if you have already awakened to the great dis-ease that the future is not the past, then *by all means*, come along with us! And if you are open to consider a new way forward, hang in here with us! We think you may in fact find the pages ahead most encouraging.

We (Beth and Paul) are Christian leadership coaches. We have worked with hundreds of leaders. We are conversant with the cutting edge of Christian ministry in places ranging from China to Germany. In the midst of all the change and the overall trajectory of decline in the West, we continue to see hope for the spiritual future of North America. Many of our clients are growing ministry in their communities. Some of them are launching new spiritual movements with the capacity for rapid multiplication and world impact, both in existing churches and in new. But they are coloring outside conventional lines—in all sorts of ways. In the world that is unfolding, thriving ministry often looks and feels really weird to those who were raised in Christendom churches and/or trained to serve them.

In this book, we work from a particular framework for understanding the social changes that are driving the North American decline of organized religion. We did not invent this framework. (We are not that smart.) But we have found it to be immensely helpful in making sense of current realities, especially to explain why some churches are thriving while most are not. Most importantly this system offers a perspective that moves us from the cliff of confusion toward a realistic hope for the new days ahead.

This framework is called Spiral Dynamics. It is a particular theory of human bio/psycho/social evolution, developed by Don Beck and Christopher Cowan, rooted in the work of Clare Graves. There are all kinds of folks across the years (philosophers, theologians, psychologists, and so forth) who have offered developmental models to explain how people and societies grow and change. We chose Spiral Dynamics for this conversation simply because we think it offers a compelling framework to explain what's going on underneath the surface of the changes we are experiencing today.

Don Beck and Christopher Cowan are co-founders of the National Values Center and authors of the 1996 book *Spiral Dynamics*. The book offers a comprehensive model of human and cultural development that allows us to better understand where we have been and where we are going. Their premise, based on four decades of research, is that human nature changes as the conditions of existence change, thus forging new systems. We change our psychology and rules for living to adapt to these new conditions. When our worldviews begin to collide with more complex life conditions, we are able to transcend the old and include the new. Both individuals and societies move along this evolutionary spiral of development, much like the major cognitive, moral, and faith developmental theories suggest.[2] This movement vacillates between expressing our individual selves to sacrificing our selves for the good of the whole. Each new system is a prelude to the next one. Both personally and corporately we can't jump levels of development; rather, we have to go through them all in a particular order. As our worldviews grow we can move up and down the spiral to meet the particular needs that our life conditions warrant.

It is important to note that these value systems are expressed in people and are not to be mistaken for types of people. They are like fractals or operating systems that point to how people think and not what they think. Each of these value systems can be expressed in both healthy and unhealthy ways. This developmental spiral is not a dominant hierarchy; rather, it is a holon (something simultaneously a whole and a part) much like the building blocks of life itself—atoms to molecules to single-cell organisms to more complex life forms that transcend and include the earlier manifestations towards more complexity. As St. Paul reminds us, the eye can never say to the hand, "I don't need you!" (1 Cor. 12: 21).

The levels of development along the spiral are color-coded for ease of application. Here are the characteristics of each, stated briefly in the order that they evolved throughout history, and also the order that human beings experience them today.

Beige began two hundred fifty thousand years ago as stone-age humans used their instincts and habits just to survive and get their basic needs met. It is a survival mentality. All humans begin at this stage at birth and can revert to this stage through illness or catastrophic disasters.

Purple began about ten thousand years ago after the end of the last major ice age when small bands of people bumped into others and had to compete for resources. As a response they formed into tribes that practiced mutual reciprocity. This self-sacrificing value system shows allegiance to the chief, elders, ancestors, and clan through rituals, magic, and superstition. The primordial stories in the early part of the Book of Genesis originated in a purple context.

Red came into existence as the safety and security needs of the tribes were met and people began questioning the superstitions and rituals of elders. This desire to be free and break away was the beginning of the egocentric system. This worldview expresses itself as impulsive, creative, and energizing as well as dominating and aggressive. It enjoys the self to the fullest without regret or guilt. Think of two-year-olds, rebellious teenagers, gangs, feudal kingdoms, contact sports, the mafia, Mardi Gras, and the Wild West.

Blue counters the lawless self-expressions of red with enforcing a code of conduct that produces stability, laws, and discipline with a healthy dose of guilt. This worldview helps to build character and moral fiber as one sacrifices the self to a transcendent cause, truth, or righteous pathway. Moses delivering the Ten Commandments on Mt. Sinai to the tribes of Israel ushers in the blue system. This value meme helps people have a fresh start as they are born again and forgiven whether or not that is within a faith tradition, a boot camp, or a 12-step group. Think of the birth of all the major faith traditions, patriotism, the Protestant work ethic, Roberts Rules of Order, and authoritarian regimes. With all blue systems, the "old and cherished ways" are the only way. Many of the "salt of the earth" people who were anchors of the communities where many of us grew up expressed healthy blue to their core. Blue worldview shows up on all ends of the spectrum in fundamentalist groups of all persuasions from quiet conservatives to atheists. When blue is fully engaged, tolerance and understanding are largely absent. Try to challenge some assumed premise of theology or politics with a person in the blue zone, and you may find them arguing back at you until they are blue in the face. Anytime that we find it unsafe or provocative to raise honest and reasonable questions about faith, we are likely experiencing a community with blue worldview.

Orange shows up once blue stabilizes the world and brings order. As this happens the focus can shift to an I-me-mine-express-myself system of achievement and personal success. This is a movement from the sacred to the secular, as witnessed with the birth of the Enlightenment and the conviction that societies prosper through reason and science. The United States was formed out of this value system. Democracy, freedom, liberty, technology, and competiveness are key. Think of the age of exploration, colonialism, the Industrial Revolution, Wall Street, the emerging middle class, Shark Tank, and the church growth movement. Key words spoken in this worldview are "free market," "profit," "entrepreneur," "strategic plan," excellence," "metrics," "purpose-driven," "and "business models." Twentieth-century New York City pastors Norman Vincent Peale and Harry Emerson Fosdick, though different theologically, pioneered a life-coaching form of preaching that has been adapted in various ways as a foundation stone for most suburban megachurches in America that live out of this worldview.

Green came onboard as people began to question the affluence and excesses of orange. Global warming, world peace, eliminating hunger, and closing the gap between the have's and have not's are important issues within this value system. The focus moves back from the individual to the larger community. Feelings, sensitivity, caring for all people, equality for all, consensus processes, and reconciliation are expressions of the green worldview. Think of the Beatles, liberation theology, feminism, LGBTQ rights, Black Lives Matter, political correctness, national healthcare, Congress of World Religions, farm-to-table food, and recycling. (Millennials are turning up green in unprecedented numbers—largely explaining why they struggle with church organizations designed for folks with blue and orange sensibilities.) When persons of green worldview choose to participate in a church it is usually because they bring with them a very positive experience with Christ from their younger years in a blue/orange kind of community. As adults, they no longer feel at home in the church where they were raised. But, somehow, they long to integrate Christian experience and identity into their adult life and worldview. Their peers, however, *if* they had no such formative experience early in life, will seldom express interest in joining them on this journey.

Yellow is the first value system that can respect all the perspectives along the spiral as healthy and needed. It can take a balcony view of all the colors along the spiral and can integrate facts, feelings, and instincts in order to help the evolutionary spiral function in a healthy way. Flexibility, spontaneity, and functionality have the highest priority. People operating in the yellow zone think and act from an inner-directed core, free to be and do as they choose. Intuition plays a key role. They not only think outside the box but also have moved outside of it as they experiment with new ideas. They are able to access knowledge on multiple levels and are comfortable with paradox, taking "both/and" perspectives. They look to chaos as a gift that helps to leverage the potential for healthy change. Think of people and organizations using chaos and systems theories, as well as experimenting with holocracy.[3] This is at present a very small percentage of Americans, estimated by Don Beck at maybe 1 percent. Look for their numbers to increase exponentially between now and midcentury. You will know them by their capacity to think beyond the confines of politically regimented thinking or behavior. They have moved out of fear and into freedom. Bible study with these folks can feel like playing in a sandbox of delight.

Turquoise experiences the wholeness of existence through mind and spirit with mystical and intuitive sensibilities. There is a growing sense that reality can be experienced, but never fully known. This value meme stands in awe of the cosmic order in which every person, species, and creature belongs. Fractals, holons, and waves are the images that help to express this connection to everything in an ecological alignment. This value meme is able to gather groups of people to work on solutions to global problems, moving beyond all the barriers of race, culture, and nation toward a global tribalism. Ego is virtually nonexistent. Think morphic fields, integral theory, evolutionary spirituality, intuitive thinking, and cooperative action. This is the most advanced value meme articulated in the Spiral Dynamics model to date, and it represents a very tiny group of people so far.

Spiral Dynamics anticipates a potentially endless array of value memes that stretch into the future mostly beyond the time horizons that we are considering in this book. It is important to note that this is the first time in history when all the colors of the spiral are bumping into each other, creating cultural wars and political polarities around the globe. It is vitally important that more people move into the second tier yellow and beyond worldviews so that we can solve the increasingly complex problems of our world.

Unless you are already very familiar with the aforementioned color code, we recommend that you make a tab or dog-ear this page so that you can come back to here as reference when you may be unclear why we are referring to one worldview or another in the pages ahead. In some cases, rereading this summary of the value memes will help readers make fuller sense of comments we make in the pages ahead.

Almost every Christian denomination was born out of a blue value system, and the middle-class American variety of church grew up in a mostly orange value system. American Christianity in the twentieth century was a mix of blue and orange and often a tug-of-war between the two. Now we are seeing that the green value system that so boisterously announced its arrival in the 1960s was not just a fad (as many church people hoped). Steadily more and more people in the United States are moving into the green worldview, following patterns observed in Europe, Canada, and Australia in recent decades. We see this most clearly expressed in the U.S. Pacific Northwest and the Northeast, where a growing number of people self-identify as "spiritual but not religious." However, in most metropolitan areas of the United States there are major pockets of green showing up, often growing from the middle of the city outward. And in the age of Internet connectedness, this is in no way limited to central-city life or to university communities.

When people move into the green value system, there is a precipitous drop in their ability and willingness to relate to blue and orange inspired systems. The percentage of green worldview people who are interested in exploring organized church is much lower than for blue and orange worldview folks. Churches that designed ministry for people in the green zone have historically shrunk or remained quite small, until recently, as more people began emerging into this worldview. The Unitarian Universalist churches have begun growing recently—for the first time in many years. Hardline fundamentalist churches are not growing as they once did; what is left of American church growth is now mostly a soft-pedaled evangelicalism, orange for all practical purposes, perfectly positioned for consumers who want a positive and practical faith experience for themselves and their kids. Most growing churches in the early twenty-first century are simply (and often brilliantly) positioning themselves to glean the dwindling supply of people who are still shopping for a good church—many of whom were raised in very blue homes.

Using Spiral Dynamics, we can see that the role of the church is not to turn "green" people "blue," but rather to partner with people, however we find them, to create that new thing that longs to spring forth. For many of the remnant church members in the conventional churches, this may be distressing, because what is unfolding simply does not look like our mother's church.

But in all times and cultures from the first century until now, the Christian gospel has found fresh expression that is both indigenous to a new time and place and also rooted in the ancient story and wisdom. We believe a gospel expression birthed in a green value system can be just as faithful as, if not more faithful than, what was birthed in the blue and orange value systems—but also weird, relative to what we have previously known. You can love Jesus at any place along the spiral.

Weird Church is divided into two sections. Primus Motus explores seven significant ministry implications that flow from the epic cultural shakeup underway from blue to orange to green to yellow value systems. For church of the Christendom variety, the shift to a green value system may feel like a cultural earthquake, shaking everything down to the foundations. You could think of these first seven chapters as aftershocks that flow from the most fundamental cultural shifts underway. But if they are aftershocks, there is nothing automatic about them—they each require leadership.

In Secundus Motus, we offer glimpses of what the immanent future will likely look like. This is not about the random flavor of the month or some clever idea one church had in Omaha. This is about the kinds of churches that will thrive in the years before us, because leaders were willing to make some difficult moves in sync with the Holy Spirit.

We do not see a uniform future as we move into the green and yellow value memes. Where blue expressions are conventional, green expressions are "multi." There are many futures, parallel futures if you will. Many churches will rise from the ashes as Christian leaders rise to the challenges of this moment in history. Some of them will be relatively orthodox theologically, with respect to past theology. Others will be highly syncretistic, blending sources and traditions that have not commonly been mixed together.

Another way of saying it would be simply: "There are many shades of weird in the church that is rising, post-Christendom." Some of them will not be your cup of tea. But one of them might surprise you and your friends, offering a newfound experience of the Holy, and very possibly in a place and manner where you least expected it.

PRIMUS MOTUS

Meta Shifts Toward the Rising Church

FOR SOME READERS, we expect that the first part of *Weird Church* will be more challenging to absorb than the second part. For other readers, we expect that these first pages will cause them to cheer, perhaps out of a sense that someone is articulating what they have been suspecting for some time. A lot depends on how much one has invested in the status quo! Conversely, a lot depends on how exasperated one is with the status quo! In almost every case where a reader finds herself struggling with the ideas in the coming pages, her adult children will struggle far less, if at all. We are leaning into the future here, into a world where our grandkids will be rising to take charge of things. Please keep this in mind.

If you are deeply invested in the trappings of your twentieth-century church experience, this may at times feel terribly painful. We get that.

The first seven chapters could be compared to "the talk" you have with your seventy-nine-year-old father-in-law when he doesn't want the heart bypass. "It's this or die, Pops." Without the seven shifts that are envisioned here, the American church will almost certainly die, except perhaps for a remnant of fringe groups who increasingly withdraw themselves and their families from the mainstream of culture. In any scenario, a smaller slice of the population is going to be involved in Christian churches in the foreseeable future than what we saw in the mid-twentieth century. But if key leaders in American Christianity do not make these shifts, we could soon be looking at a Christian future as grim as what we currently see in Scandinavia. That is the future that we do not want. And we would underline: that future can be avoided!

With these shifts, the church will morph, dancing with the Holy Spirit into its next chapters and iterations. With these shifts, beautiful things happen. New discoveries, breakthroughs, and reformations are possible, if not likely. This is why we are both so hopeful about the future of faith in North America.

We recommend that you read the Primus Motus chapters one at a time. Take some time after each to put the book down. You may want to journal about feelings and ideas that the chapter elicits in you. Or you may just want to give it a few hours, and go about your business, letting it soak in. You may find that some chapters are very easy to process and others leave you troubled. That's fine. You may come to somewhat different conclusions as to the nature of the shift required. That's wonderful, because it is a sign that you are thinking deeply and asking good questions.

Whether you are reading *Weird Church* with a study group or processing it solo, we recommend to you the free downloadable study guide that is available both from the publisher (www.thepilgrimpress.org) and from www.epicentergroup.org. Even if you find yourself hooked and reading quickly through this book, we urge you to take time to be still and process.

Because the biggest question for you, the reader, is not "What will the church look like in 2050?" More relevant would be the questions "Where am I in this future?" and "What shifts am I called to make in order to travel with God toward this future?"

FROM FEAR TO FREEDOM

God of change and glory, God of time and space, when

we fear the future, give to us your grace. . . . As the old ways

disappear, let your love cast out all fear.

—AL CARMINES, 1973

In every time and place, across the centuries and continents, each of us has to work with the context where life has dropped us. For all that we would love to control in life, none of us will ever be able to choose the moment that we are born, nor the era and historical setting. Some folks were born into Damascus or Baghdad in the early twenty-first century, surrounded by bombings and chaos in their formative years. Others were born into quiet and stable villages where all of life's fundamental needs were graciously met. Imagine how different life can look to any of us depending upon just this one variable: When and where were you born? To what epoch of history were you committed without any personal vote on the matter? And to what sacred stories were you introduced? It is true not only about our childhoods, but also, for those of us in Christian ministry, it is true about the time and place in which we are called to share and live the gospel with our contemporaries. Some things are simply chosen for us.

Almost all of us reading this book have drawn as our lot the early decades of this crazy century. We can wish for another age further back or further forward in time. We can try to escape into those rare social contexts that still remain relatively insulated from postmodernity. But such places are disappearing faster than the glaciers. We are called to play as best we can the cards we were dealt in North America 2015–2050.

One of those cards that we have been dealt is an extremely anxious and fearful age—extending far beyond the world of religion. (Okay, it probably is not as fearful as the years of Black Plague. But even in those years, there may have been more stability in world order and worldview than what we have currently.) Especially if we were born before 1975, so much of the world that we first knew is shifting on us. This seismic season has been underway for most of our lives. It is a moment of history that William Bridges would surely classify as liminal space, a transitional era: days of in-between.[4]

Any time we have a transition between organizational leaders, between college and first job, between a positive pregnancy test and the birth of the child, between bad diagnosis and death—we may experience liminal time. During this season of in-between, significant old ways and assumptions may fade, long before the new things to come are fully apparent— leaving us caught in the middle. We find ourselves simultaneously grieving a world that is gone with the wind and seeking to adjust to that which is dawning.

At this current moment of history, we see enormous shifts—in the nature of the world economy; in the nature of work, profession, and career; in the nature of family relationships; in the nature of technology as it relates to every nuance of daily life; and (of course) in the nature of community. This is a lot of change all at once.

Seventeen centuries of Christendom reached an end sometime just before the year 2000. And yet because so many of our constituents have been formed spiritually, intellectually, and socially in the twilight of Christendom, many churches have often been able to get away with a basic continuance of twentieth-century ways of thinking and doing until today, albeit with steadily shrinking and aging constituencies. This remnant afterglow is all about to end in much of the United States—though you can add a few more years in parts of the southeastern and south central United States and some other traditional pockets.

Two towering realities now force us to face the full truth of the death of Christendom: First, the rise of a new generation of adults who are largely disengaged with Christendom-shaped church communities and, second, the rising "death tsunami"[5] of the elders that have kept old-school churches in business for years after their time expired. By the year 2050, most of "church-as-we-have-known-it" will almost certainly no longer exist. For those who are deeply invested in institutional forms of Christianity, this is perhaps one more reason to join the politicians and the culture warriors in their fearful stupor. The thought that a world might be unfolding where only a small sliver of the population is interested in Christian church membership sends cold chills down our spines.

And yet that is the world that is coming, and quickly.

All the mania around church metrics and the obsession over ministry tweaks are driven largely by fear—a panic reflex to turn back time. The continued orange worldview fixation on measuring "vital signs" of a healthy late-Christendom church is doing nothing to change the score. And those church leaders who have moved to green or yellow value systems (and who are perhaps most ready to lead us well into the decades ahead) are so turned off and discouraged by the metrics-mania that many are exiting church leadership at the very moment when we need them the most! These talented and discouraged would-be leaders know that the stuff we compulsively measure at church (like that which we compulsively measure in our public schools) is often irrelevant to God's best future.

Many of the denominational conversations around "church revitalization" do not begin to contemplate how different the future of vital churches will be compared to the past. Too often, we try to coach aging churches how to make a happy version of 1995 feebly work again for a few more years. Too often, with our new churches, we expect our planters to mobilize people to join a religious club and pay for services like folks used to do. And when they don't, how quickly we are ready to pull the plug on the project rather than rethink how to create resilient twenty-first-century faith communities. Much of what passes for judicatory leadership today looks to us to be based in our collective reptilian brain: "fight, flight, freeze, and eat the kids!" Judicatories, for the most part, find themselves stuck in a state of fear. In this state their options are limited to fighting for what was, trying out the latest business fads as a way forward, acting as if nothing has changed, and killing any attempts at innovation under the guise of it not fitting into their structures and processes. In a concerted and noble effort to stem the tide of decline through high control they end up suffocating innovation and the movement of the Holy Spirit.

But yesterday is gone. It is not coming back.

Naming this reality may actually help some of us to stop hyperventilating and to start leading again. It might help us to realize that many strategies that served us well in the late twentieth century will not serve us well in the future.

Better that we face reality and name our fears than to live in denial and suppose that, by praying or working harder or coming up with better worship services, somehow our church can make yesterday's strategies work again.

Have you ever been in an elevator and stopped to imagine what would happen if the power went out and you were stuck with a group of strangers for hours on end? You would likely end up sitting on the floor in the dark, as each person tells his or her respective story. Such stranded elevator moments would help some of us who lead churches to get in touch with the broader sea of fear—the fear of death, of job loss, of harm to our children; the fear of a world that does not understand us or appreciate us, let alone love us; the fear that somehow we are not worthy of love or blessing. Get a climate scientist in the stranded elevator and almost every fear we could articulate about church health will pale before the hard realities of what is about to happen to life on this planet if water temperatures continue to rise unabated.

Deep listening to our neighbors may help us put our fears about the future of institutional religion in proper perspective, and might even leave us feeling a bit shallow in terms of the stuff we obsess about. Neighbors are a gift for helping us keep some perspective.

We believe the good news for this era is rooted in the story of Pentecost. It is good news for the whole world. But the church leaders need it as much as anyone these days!

After the unspeakable tragedy and horror of Jesus' execution, a shell-shocked group of followers still hung together. They were a mess: a mixture of memories of this Jesus story or that Jesus saying, memories of the magical moments when thousands were fed, when lepers were made whole. But the Roman Empire, in collusion with the local religious establishment, had crushed them. Killed Jesus. Many of them had experienced unexplainable visions and encounters with Jesus in the weeks since his death, but after about a month, the weird encounters had ceased. No one had seen Jesus for more than ten days. Even the tales of Jesus' ascension into the sky seemed surreal. Under this much stress, everyone was feeling a little crazy. Wild rumors abounded. No one knew fully who could be believed. Grieving and wishful thinking were as much alive as any experiences of a risen Christ. To say the band of followers were *afraid* some fifty days after Easter would be a gross understatement. *Numb* would probably more accurately describe the mood.

By Luke's account, 120 of them were locked into a room somewhere in Jerusalem. Windows were closed and the mood, somber. We can conjecture that for each one who remained, several others had left. Easter seemed now like a dream, a mass hallucination. An extraordinarily magical season was over. Or so it seemed. It was the mother of liminal moments.

And it was in this moment and in this place where the Weird Thing happened.

Air began to move in the room, first a subtle breeze, then a wind, blowing in a room with closed windows, almost two millennia before HVAC. Those dozing were awakened. And then the fire roared—flames dancing on their heads. And the languages flourished—the ability to speak to anyone present in the city during an international festival, without Rosetta Stone.

The people who had followed Jesus had seen their share, by now, of very strange days. But this one took the cake.

Wind and fire were symbols of the presence of God, well known in the Hebrew tradition. Of course, in the craziness of the moment, it is debatable how obvious this would have been to those present. But for those who took in the whole cascade of events on this most bizarre Sunday, a few things were immediately clear. The Jesus followers were suddenly filled with poise and power. They were communicating with people who should not have understood much of what they were saying. And by afternoon, they were baptizing people, lots of people. Luke's estimate was about three thousand human beings.

There was no strategic plan, no bishops, and no butts in seats.

If there were one Bible story that you could travel back and experience first-hand, would not Pentecost be your pick? It is definitely up there with the crossing of the Red Sea. Almost everything that matters to us at this critical moment of history finds it roots in this mysterious and amazing day.

Regardless of how you picture what literally happened that day, further reflection would suggest:

◆ The Christian movement found its groove that day.

◆ It was the act of God, and not in any way dependent on human effort or faith.

◆ Jesus had kept his promise to come back to those who loved him— although there will forever be debate as to whether the coming of the Spirit was the fulfillment of Jesus' promise to come again or simply the fulfillment of his cryptic talk of a Comforter who would come.

While this day had significant historical meaning for the start of the Christian movement, we believe it is also an archetypal day—a day that defines God's relationship with humanity in all times and places. Pentecost happens intermittently across the centuries. Whenever good people are living in liminal space, it is in exactly that moment that Pentecost is apt to occur.

In the wake of this Weird Thing, the Jesus movement began to spread and to innovate on the fly; creativity came to life.

Even as many twentieth-century churches fall into ruins, something wonderful is coming. If God is in it, it is going to be good. Much of what is coming is going to stretch our current imagination. And it will look and feel weird to those with blue and orange sensibilities. But the Holy Spirit of Christ will surely anchor us in this riotous liminal season and help to bring birth to the new things God desires for our age. For all that is passing away, the Pentecost experience offers the promise that, wherever the Spirit is, greater things are yet to come.

The most important shift in us, however, in order to fully let go of the past and embrace this wild and wonderful future, is to be filled with the power and peace that the Spirit offers. We simply cannot enter the land God is preparing if we are frozen up in fear.

"Perfect love casts out fear" (1 John 4:18).

Where ministry is taking root and thriving in the green and yellow value zones, the leaders are remarkably calm and embracing of the world where they have been called to serve. We work with many of these leaders. Judicatory leaders may misinterpret their calm as a lack of urgency. Look closer and you may discover that these leaders have a deeper sense of urgency than most of their peers—and that the urgency expands exponentially beyond concerns of church institutional metrics. These leaders of this new brand have to remind themselves constantly that some of the megachurches still thriving around them are working with a different population than they are, in terms of the worldview. But given the trend lines, it is important that they stick with their commitment to people living in the green and emerging into yellow value systems. They are pioneers. If they don't figure out ministry in this new social terrain, who will?

These leaders understand that no church can control the people who are rising to adult consciousness; they are free spiritual agents. They will make their own covenants, establish their own ground rules, create their own customized disciplines and rituals. People in green consciousness are not going to wait for a card-carrying clergy person to break bread and share the cup. They are not going to wait for a church pledge card in order to begin giving back in profound ways. They are simply not going to comply with many of our institutional habits and demands—these people are free agents *and they know it.*

And yet this new-found freedom from all things institutional is not necessarily a guarantee of an ever more fragmented future. The future is going to feel really fragmented for the next few decades, if you understand unity as primarily organizational/institutional. From the church to the U.S. Congress to the United Nations, fragmentation is our current reality within almost every institution.

And yet, step outside the institution for a moment, and possibilities become apparent that you couldn't see locked inside. When the Spirit wind blows, people are woven together in new ways and alliances that only God can envision—in ways that only God can design. Unity is not an organizational challenge so much as a gift of Spirit to humankind. On the day in the fall of 2015 that Pope Francis gave his riveting address to a joint session of the U.S. Congress, you did not have to be Catholic or sign on to all that the Pope believes to feel a universal connection to his message and moral invitation. Spirit winds were blowing.

Most of the Protestant denominational structures that we know in the West will crumble between now and 2050, due to loss of funding and/or to unending conflict. By midcentury, there may still be a few bureaucrats huddled in merged judicatory offices here and there, but the glory will have departed—if ever there was glory in such places. Any ecumenism or plan for unity that is mostly organizational will be utterly irrelevant when the covenanting organizations evaporate, simply a pitiful consolidation of antiquated forms into one unified sinking ship.

The Holy Spirit has a better future for us! Better than we could ever design or organize on our own!

God is already alive in 2050, waiting for us in our future, a future of beautiful alliances beyond our foggiest imagination. And as we set our feet firmly onto that steadily emerging Spirit reality and dare to abide there, we shall be empowered. As a rising tide of people, secular and religious, emerge into yellow consciousness, all things spiritual will look different to us than when we dwelled all those years in a land of orange and green.

Remember, yellow consciousness is about a balcony view. It opens us up to discern the beauty and brilliance in all things. There could be a rediscovery of Scripture by midcentury that will rival the Great Awakenings. That rediscovery almost certainly will embrace more than simply the Old and New Testaments. It will likely include the Bhagavad Gita and the Koran. But a major awakening is so very possible—barely imaginable to us in the muck and mire of our current fretting and obsessing—and eventually, nearly inevitable!

How many pastors have sat with an elderly woman in the hours after her husband of fifty-plus years has vanished from life? A part of her has died with him. It is a place of disorientation. It is hard to see forward toward anything good from that bleak spot. Yet how many of those same pastors have observed that same person three years later, looking younger than ever, taking a cruise with the grandkids, sometimes remarried, and having the time of her life? God is good. Human beings are wired to be resilient. And the future is never fully defined by present circumstances, no matter how overwhelming they may seem in the moment.

It is a season for radical trust in God and for waiting. Waiting for the Spirit to fall upon us. There is freedom to be found in the place of hope and trust. Recall the witness of the Prophets, seeing fulfillment and hope, when all seemed to be lost. Remember Jesus' vision of the kingdom of God, a mad vision of a world of grace and kindness cast at a time and place where the kingdom of the world they knew was cruel beyond the capacity of words to describe. One could make the case, when you cook down all of the spiritual practices, and bulldoze the real estate, that the core of our faith is living and acting out of radical and ridiculous trust in that good future, not yet revealed, that God has prepared for God's people.

The writer of the first Epistle of Peter echoes to us, the spiritual descendants of the first-century Jesus-followers: "You are a chosen race, a royal priesthood, a holy nation, a people for God's possession" (1 Pet. 2:9).

Do we believe this? Would we dare to risk believing this? If we don't fully believe this, what's the value in trying to hold the church together, anyway? Either we believe God is alive and creating a new future with human beings, building on the spiritual foundations of biblical faith—or not. And if God is doing this, it is not incumbent on us to understand how it's going to all fit together. It *is* incumbent on us to dare to cast aside our fear, let go of our need to control the outcome, and put our hope in God.

As we dare to trust and to hope, a sweet freedom awaits each of us, emancipating us from the fearfulness of our age.

FROM SETTLED CAMP TO
SHALOM ON THE MOVE

You will receive power when the Holy Spirit has

come upon you; and you will be my witnesses in Jerusalem,

in all Judea and Samaria, and to the ends of the earth.

—ACTS 1:8

What if you and ten of your closest friends were told by Jesus that it was up to you to be witnesses to the love of God in your community, your region, your country, to the ends of the world? How would you go about doing that if you had to start from scratch? No defined program. No curriculum. No paradigm. No home office. Certainly no direct deposit and no W-2s.

This was the predicament the Apostles faced as they waited upon the Spirit in Jerusalem after Jesus' ascension into heaven. They had no idea how they were going to do this nor had they much confidence that they could pull it off. They did their best by having a committee meeting and drawing straws to fill out their vacated apostle position. In fear they hunkered down until the Spirit of God blew open the shutters and their hearts at Pentecost, attuning them to Christ-consciousness in real time. After that, everything they did was done through deep listening to where the Spirit was guiding them and trusting in that guidance even when she stretched them beyond their comfort zones—which was nearly every day.

It was through the diaspora of Christian refugees after the stoning of Stephen that the witness spread from Jerusalem to Judea. It was after Peter had three visions telling him to eat "unclean" food that the witness spread through Samaria via an "unclean" Gentile family that Peter visited and baptized. It was through hitchhiking a chariot ride on a dangerous and deserted road that Phillip met and baptized an Ethiopian eunuch and the witness spread to the ends of the world, which for the earliest Christians was Africa. It was through Ananias that Paul, a known persecutor of Jesus followers, was healed of his blindness only to become the greatest Christian missionary of the first century, taking the stories of Jesus all over the Mediterranean region. There was no strategic plan or program curriculum for any of this. These Christian pioneers were simply watching and listening for where Christ was showing up and then courageously journeying into the unknown to meet and obey the Spirit's call.

The Book of Acts is filled with these weird stories, collected from the early church during a season when it was still a "hold-on-to-the-seat-of-your-pants" movement. At that time there were no specific gathering places for Christians. Certainly there was no "Sunday at 11." They gathered in homes or in synagogues, sometimes in secret. The word for "church" in Greek, *ekklesia*, and Latin, *ecclesia*, means "a called out people of God." The early church was a community of believers "called out of the mainstream" to a weird enterprise. They risked everything for the sake of sacrificial love in a world dominated by a red worldview, where they looked like the crazy ones.

However, within a few centuries this marginal movement became more settled within the social order of the Roman Empire. The temples that housed Roman Gods were converted into Christian cathedrals. These sacred spaces served as reminders of God's presence in the community as well as gathering places for rituals during holy days. In short order, "church" became associated more with the building that housed religious services than with the radical movement that was based out of such places. Within just a few generations, the whole enterprise was so tamed that there was little radical or weird about it anymore. It became the new normal in most of Europe. And we might add that it was a normal increasingly un-aligned with the original Jesus movement.

Every century or so, little renewal movements within the Catholic Church would rock the boat, embracing anew the weirdness of gospel community. But for the most part these revivals never tampered with the sleepy, predictable, banal, and blue-worldview religion that Christianity had become for the illiterate majority of Europeans.

At first this European style of Christianity did not transplant well in the United States. We did not have enough trained clergy, for one thing. And an ocean's separation from the established religious powers of Europe allowed for more free thinking, more diversification, and more audacity to take things into our own hands. From moms who baptized their own children to entrepreneurs who just started preaching and made up their own church, the early Americans marched to a different beat. What had begun as a wild movement out to the ends of the earth found some degree of renaissance in America seventeen centuries later as a movement from house to house. The American Great Awakenings further helped to stamp a high value on individual experience and upon the compelling authority of an individual's experience with Christ.

However, in the nineteenth century, as people moved into cities and modes of transportation improved, distinctively American, institutional Christendom churches began to proliferate across the continent. House churches gave way to brush arbors, which gave way to increasingly elaborate church buildings for worship services and Christian education. The focus was on building up the gathered community to provide ways for people to learn about the faith and practice ways of loving God and our neighbors as we love ourselves.

In some churches, there was an added emphasis on personal experiences of conversion and/or Spirit anointing. But once folks had collected their desired experiences, the latter churches rolled mostly like the others: focused on education and a somewhat prescribed set of faith practices.

Many of us came to faith in such places. It is not our intent to disparage settled-church-in-a-building. But we do want to note that this shift eventually became complicit in the decline of many North American churches.

Within such Christian communities, there is often a palpable sense of belovedness where one can be known and embraced, warts and all, from birth to death. Christians understand that community has the power to bring healing and wholeness in mysterious ways through embodied grace. In this sense the community becomes the lived-out sacrament of Christ's body broken for the world.

Even if such communities sometimes become a bit clubby and hard for an outsider to enter, they often make significant investments in the world outside their tight circle. In particular, the church's outward expression of its beliefs and values seeks to enhance a sense of stability and constancy in the culture. American churches often became the outposts of hope in any kind of disaster, providing food, clothing, shelter, and volunteers on the ground. However, as church attendance declines in North America, the capacity of churches to support such ministries will diminish.[6]

Most Christians today know that the church is not a building, but rather the gathered people sent by God into the world. Nonetheless, we have kept our focus upon gathering people into the building for as long as any of us can remember.[7]

The building traffic is typically directed toward a variety of programs, starting with the worship service. In busy buildings, ancillary programs may run the gamut from support groups to knitting groups, basketball teams to preschools, food pantries to confirmation classes. Budgets are built. The best people we can find are hired to run these programs. To be successful, the church gets on the never-ending sustainability wheel of recruiting charismatic staff to attract more people by creating ever more engaging programming in order to pay for the building and the payroll.

Almost every church considers itself friendly, with doors wide open, hoping that people will show up for services and programs the way they used to show up. But, as churches age and cultures shift, fewer and fewer churches are able to get the building traffic. Fewer still are able to translate good building traffic into growing worship attendance and donations sufficient to pay for all the staff and the facilities. In the decades ahead, the denominationally based, program-oriented, building-centered church will near extinction (except, of course, where there is endowment money to prop it up).

In all the current frenzy to "revitalize" these sinking ships, church leaders are rarely pausing to ask if this is the most efficacious way to cultivate people in the Way of Jesus in an increasingly post-Christian world. An increasing majority of North Americans have little connection with or desire for faith formation, worship services, or busyness in a cottage industry of never-ending programs and activities sponsored by local churches.

In repeated consultations with declining congregations, we hear the tales of the days when the halls and rooms of the church building were full of people attending church programming. Their halls are often now very quiet and dimly lit by modern standards, depressing even to church people. The adjoining rooms where children once gathered now store random clutter and hand-me-down donations, awaiting sale at the annual bazaar, where money will be raised to help pay for the aging facility.

Clay Shirky, a respected voice on the social and economic implications of Internet technologies, says that when a movement becomes an institution its primary concern becomes self-preservation. He refers to the 80/20 rule, which states that 20 percent of the users of any institution use 80 percent of the resources. The 80 percent zone is the cost of running the institution, while 20 percent of users are treated as employees, whether paid or unpaid. An institution by its very nature always excludes and marginalizes people. The focus shifts to a consumer mentality that tries to keep church attenders happy so that they will give money so that 20 percent of the leaders can be employed doing the work of the church. As this happens, decisions are made that benefit fewer and fewer people and we lose the bigger picture of sharing the good news that God's kingdom is at hand. We can end up playing church more than being the church.[8]

A rising wave of green-worldview Christians are asking: Is any of this really what Jesus had in mind when he empowered his disciples to be witnesses of God's love to the ends of the earth?

We are told in the Gospels that Jesus began his ministry by inviting people to follow him. Jesus formed an intentional community with a group of twelve men and several women whom he mentored in the way of *metanoia*, a transformative change of heart. Jesus lived in community and taught his followers that community is important for their own transformation. But he also taught them that God is always on the move.

The story of Jesus sending seventy people out of their comfort zones into unknown communities as strangers seeking welcome in chapter 10 of Luke's Gospel offers a compelling alternative vision to most of today's churches. It epitomizes the shift from church as a building with programs to forming a community sent by God into the world.

Samaria was known as an unfriendly territory with a history of animosity toward the Jews. Samaritans were known to have an indifference to God language and a cool contempt for judgmental religious neighbors trying to preach religion to them—much like our postmodern culture today. And yet it is here, of all places, that Jesus sent out his apprentices. The very act of sending them out was a process of shaping them as disciples as well as providing them with a model for what faithfulness to Jesus' way of life looks like.

In this story Jesus tells them first to pray, reminding them that they can do nothing without the guidance of the Spirit. Then he tells them to leave their baggage—their need for control, power, safety, and security—behind. They were to depend solely upon God to guide them on their journey into the unknown. Deep listening was required—both to God and to the communities where they were sent. In their listening and discerning, they were to keep an eye out for "people of peace—folks who welcomed and helped them, and who might serve as gateways into the community.

They were sent as the strangers who were to seek welcome with people who were willing to share their gifts with them. The heart of the shift that Jesus models is this: They were not called to welcome the stranger; rather, they were called to *be* the stranger seeking welcome. As they became the stranger, they grew in their capacities to heal the sin that separates people from each other, from God, from all sentient beings. When they looked into the eyes of the other they could see their own humanity reflected. They in turn grew in compassion. It is the palpable experience of holy witness, divine presence, heaven on earth.

This is the opposite image of church people standing at the door with smiles and brochures luring people onto their own turf. The seventy are put in a humble position of powerlessness. They are sent to be solely dependent on people they have not yet met. It turns on its head our concept of being a welcoming and friendly church that ministers to willing customers.

It is exactly at the point of trusting enough to let go that the disciples were able to truly seek people and places that welcomed them. When they found these people of peace they were to get to know them, eat with them, and form relationships of trust. Jesus specifically told them to eat whatever was placed in front of them even if it was ritually unclean. Again, this was a radical request to be willing to go beyond long-observed religious and cultural law and customs in order to embody shalom. This was quite a departure from the doctrinal issues and infighting among the Pharisees. It is precisely when we embrace our common humanity that we are opened to the kind of grace that heals miraculously. We are made whole when we become part of the infinite unfolding of God's love in the world.

Then almost as an afterthought, but with deliberate emphasis, Jesus says, "Before you leave, share with them that together you have witnessed the kingdom of God." It was an invitation to wake up to the ultimate truth of existence: The realm of God is within, is right here, right now.

This may be vaguely familiar to some of us. We may have been a part of summer mission trips to poor communities, where we experienced hospitality from strangers and perhaps even experienced a call to lifetime ministry. Youth summer mission trips have been turning young people and their sponsors upside down for years. Then we come home to consumer church-in-the-building again, and we feel a huge disconnect.

There is so much to reclaim in the story of Jesus sending the seventy as a way forward in our postmodern, post-Christendom culture where the majority of people are either done with church or have no experience with it. The beauty of this approach is that it is light. It is organic. It is simple. It is not about heavy-duty organizational development or months of planning to launch something new. This practice is not something to check off a to-do list in a month; rather, it is a way of being and doing that transforms all involved over time. And the way of being/doing works with or without programs.

There will be programs, until the end of time. They will come, they will morph, they will go. Human beings habitually organize life into deliverables. It's fine. But the program du jour is always secondary! Program was secondary in the first century, and it is the same in the twenty-first. The relational adventure that Jesus modeled *is* foundational. The practice of unconventional relationship is the core to our way of life—the practice of countercultural values in community! Without that, we have nothing that will last. Without that, there is little point in getting more people into our buildings.

Jesus turns program on its head, and invites a church of practice. "Can we, the church, hang with you and will you hang with us? Will you welcome us into your world? Will you allow us to sit at your table? Will you allow us to learn about you—your joys, sorrows, aspirations, and gifts? And who knows, maybe in the process we will discover the Christ in each other."

Donna Claycomb Sokol is a pastor in downtown Washington, D.C. As she meditated with a group of friends on Luke 10, she immediately thought of the persons in her church who are unhoused: those who live in shelters or on the sidewalk. These persons have no physical place in which to welcome her. But almost immediately, she realized that they invite her into their stories instead. It is a magnificent metaphor, universally applicable: People's stories are like virtual tiny houses. Imagine yourself entering into this holiest of places, at the behest of another, who dares to trust you. Entering into their story, taking off your shoes, sitting down, breaking bread, sharing tea, and lingering there as long as they give you welcome. No rushing off to the next place. Rather, slowing down, abiding there, honoring them, honoring their story as a place *more than good enough* to rank as destination—and not just a place en route to another more important agenda.

Jesus invites us to meet and to dwell with people where they are. To listen deeply for the presence of God in their stories and to give witness to the sacrament of life unfolding around us with every breath we take. The relationship must not be commoditized as a means toward growing worship attendance or membership. A Jesus-style encounter is simply that—an encounter. Community for the sake of community! Jesus invites us to discover together the sacredness of this moment and to share that experience with others.

In God's counterculture we break bread together, we laugh and weep together, and we learn together until we finally arrive at a sense of one-another-ness, interconnectedness. The New Testament word for this is *koinonia*. We should note that in its ordinary Greek usage, it was not a religious word—it just meant "common table fellowship." Yet such community is often anything but common. It becomes transformational and holy when the Spirit of God shows up at the table.

When we truly show up to one another at common tables, in the power of the Holy Spirit, we become a healing balm for each other and the world around us. When we practice deep listening, we are changed—both us and our neighbors. The Spirit births in us new initiatives, new understandings, new possibilities, new hope. The word "shalom" seems to encapsulate this hope of wholeness for individuals, communities, and the whole world. As such community forms, others will be drawn to its magic and will in turn be more open to explore the depths of their own spirituality. To borrow Jesus' words from another Gospel, "Seek first the kingdom of God, and all these other things will be added to you" (Matt. 6:33 NKJV).

When the seventy returned they were filled with tales that surprised even them. As they journeyed into the unknown they grew in their trust of the unfolding of the Spirit, sensing that God was in them and with them, even in times of fear and doubt. They learned that sometimes it is okay to shake the dust off and move on. And they discovered that when we seek welcome, we often find the kingdom of God as plain as day.

As they reported back to Jesus and to one another, reflecting on their experiences, they experienced true worship. Worship in this most primitive of churches was not an intellectual download of information, a faith-based pep talk or an ecstatic emotional escape from normal existence; rather, it was a joy-filled witness to the God-things that were happening in their lives, the unfolding of the kingdom of God, right there in their very neighborhood.

The disciples exclaimed, "We saw [other] people casting out demons in your name." Jesus responded, "All the same, the great triumph is not in your authority over evil, but in God's authority over you and presence with you. Not what you do for God but what God does for you—that's the agenda for rejoicing" (Luke 10:20 MSG).

This journey into Samaria provided a way for Jesus to shape his disciples. A disciple of Jesus begins with prayer and the vulnerability that comes with being a stranger. A disciple of Jesus trusts in the unfolding of grace and curiously looks for it everywhere. A disciple of Jesus looks for people of peace and befriends them. A disciple of Jesus offers the potential for healing through community. A disciple of Jesus shares the unfolding of shalom in the midst of community, proclaiming like Jacob in the wilderness as he set up his stone altar, "Surely the Lord is in this place and I did not know it, this is none other than the house of God and the gate of heaven."

This movement outside the church walls is risky. It takes a courageous leap of faith, especially for the 20 percent of church users most heavily invested in the current model of ministry focused on life inside the building.

So what would a church on the move look like in the twenty-first century?

Broadway Church in Indianapolis is one compelling example. They have redefined what it means to serve their urban community by seeing their neighbors as children of God. In a counterintuitive—leave your baggage behind—move, they stopped their food pantry, clothing ministry, after-school program, and summer youth program. They hired a "roving listener," to rove the neighborhood, block by block, spending time with the neighbors in order to better understand the gifts, passions, hopes, and dreams of their neighborhood. They moved away from a caregiver role into a community organizing practice.

Instead of asking, "What can I do for you?" they ask questions like these:

♦ "What three things do you do well enough that you could teach others how to do them?"

♦ "What three things would you like to learn?"

◆ Who, besides God and me, is going with you along the way?"

De'Amon Harges, the "roving listener," began connecting people with common interests. One example is the farmer's market that was birthed from forty-five backyard gardeners who live within four blocks of the church. Harges first brought them together around a meal with no agenda. As the gardeners met monthly they began to realize that they had something valuable to share. Ordinary meal became eschatological meal when their awareness of God's preferred future emerged around the tables. It was not programmed. Now their passion for gardening is meeting a deep need in their neighborhood, helping to heal an urban food desert.

De'Amon says, "Broadway has died to its old self, giving up the things that were holding it back. The church's resurrection has come from seeking the gifts of others. Our role in this place is to become like yeast— that invisible agent for social change. It is not about us as an agency inviting people to witness God here. Instead, what we want to do is to see God out of this place."[9]

There are many examples of communities that are living into this "shalom on the move" all over the United States, from John Helmiere at Valley and Mountain fellowship in South Seattle, who entered his mission field by getting off a bus and living as a homeless person for four days, to Hannah Terry in Houston, Texas, who moved into a low-income housing complex and formed the Fondren Apartment Ministry, an intentional community with refugees from Africa.

Church as movement listens to the heartbeat of the community and is highly contextual. The community is constantly discerning where Christ is already at work and then asking how they can partner with that. They trust that the Spirit of God will always be found where there is light, love, energy, passion, and hope in the neighborhood. They recognize that the power of the gospel and the assets already alive in the neighborhood are more critical than the church's buildings, money, and status within the judicatory. Those whose hearts are attuned are able to ride this wave of grace instead of pushing a boulder of programs up the proverbial hill.

Church as movement is light, nimble, contextual, organic, creative, collaborative, and easily accessible—either via an inquirer or via someone with something to share. It meets people where they are and invites them to contribute as much or as little as they like out of a sense of abundance. It sees everyday life and discipleship formation in a unified vision. It is about small groups of people getting together to dream about God's preferred future for them and their neighborhoods and then daring to make that a reality. It is ultimately about trusting that we and our neighbors, together, *are* enough and *have* enough to make the critical journey towards the realization of God's dreams for us.

FROM THE ILLUSION
OF A CHRISTIAN SOCIETY TO
CHRISTIAN SUBVERSION

"Who put you in charge here? What business do you have doing this?"...

The religious leaders realized these two [Peter and John] were laymen with

no training in scripture or formal education. . . . They warned them that

they were on no account ever again to speak or teach in the name of Jesus.

But Peter and John spoke right back, "Whether it's right in God's eyes to

listen to you rather than to God, you decide. As for us, there's no question—

we can't keep quiet about what we've seen and heard."

—ACTS 4:7–20 MSG

The Christian story and movement was birthed out of values and practices that subverted an empire. It was a rebellion that turned power on its head. The nature of the threat was certainly not lost upon the Romans, who proceeded quickly to execute the founder of the movement. To be followers of The Way of Jesus was considered an act of treason against the empire's pagan gods, and Christians were often perse-cuted because of it.

Jesus embodied his radical message through actions: touching lepers, eating with the lost, and healing the socially outcast. He elaborated on that message through his stories and sermons. Those who are last will be first. Blessed are the peacemakers and the persecuted. Love your enemies. Whenever you feed the poor, clothe the naked, or visit the prisoner, you are embracing God in them.

In the earliest sources, we clearly see that it's mostly poor people, peo-ple with physical challenges, prostitutes, people with addictions, tax col-lectors, and the party crowd—those on the bottom and the outside—who really hear Jesus' teaching and respond to him. It's the leaders and insiders (both within the government and the religious institutions) who crucify him. Jesus ultimately died a humiliating and torturous death on the cross because he posed a threat to the political and religious powers.

In the decades after Jesus' brief ministry in Palestine, the Christian movement exploded across the Roman Empire. This movement was shaped and formed by the same subversive practices: caring for the wid-ows, healing the sick, sharing what the people had in common, and teach-ing the ways of love and peace. Jesus' apostles were constantly getting in trouble with the religious leaders and power brokers of their day by these simple acts. They were beaten, jailed, and finally killed because this way of life was such a threat to the social and political order.

About the term "kingdom of God." Jesus was very careful in his choice of words. The term spooked the Romans. It very likely also spooked the folks for whom "kingdom" was always bad news. "Kingdom" in Jesus' time always connoted totalitarian abuse and an utter lack of care for the individual. So the kingdom of the tender-loving God who cares for each creature—this is really an "un-kingdom." It is a play on words—the most sobering of ironies, the ultimate oxymoron. In recent times, out of a concern for nonsexist language, many Christians have stopped using the term "kingdom." We respect this, but we have chosen to take this brutal and of-fensive term as Jesus gave it, so that we also can experience its full shock value and ironic power.

At the beginning of the fourth century, things abruptly changed. The Roman Empire was feeling increasingly threatened by rising forces beyond its border. In CE 311 the Romans became more open minded about matters of religion. Novel (and desperate) idea: pray to any God if it can help us hold back the barbarians! Christians were granted an indulgence and asked to pray "to their God for our safety, for that of the republic, and for their own, that the commonwealth may continue uninjured on every side, and that they may be able to live securely in their homes."[10] This was the first step in creating an alliance with the Christian God, whom Constantine considered the strongest deity. Two years later, in CE 313, Constantine issued the Edict of Milan decriminalizing Christian worship. At that time he was more concerned about social stability and the protection of the empire from the wrath of the Christian God than he was for justice or care for the Christians. Finally the emperor consolidated his power within the church when he convened the first worldwide gathering of Christian leaders at the Council of Nicaea in CE 325.[11]

Christendom was born.

The Jesus movement was subsumed into the empire and "Christian disciple" became synonymous with "good citizen." It all happened so fast, and without the aid of cable news. Christians didn't see it coming and were not able to comprehend fully what was going on. In the centuries since that fateful moment in Western history, our churches have become repositories of shaping and forming good citizens with moral education, law, and order. Seventeen hundred years later, across the Atlantic from old Rome, many American churches still display the U.S. flag prominently and close to the altar as an enduring symbol that patriotism and Christianity are one in the same. (And if not one and the same, they are kissing cousins.) "God Bless America" continues to be the unifying statement of American political leaders and a pacifying salve for the masses.

Most churches today mirror political institutions in structure, operation, and governance. Denominations gather to vote on doctrine and polity and, in some cases, to elect bishops to oversee the church. Likewise, pastors are trained and carefully credentialed to administer the sacraments and manage their churches. Rebellion in this paradigm is when a church chooses to withhold financial support from the denomination or when pastors break the moral codes found in the bylaws. "Don't rock the boat" is the underlying narrative. Few American churches cultivate a feisty subversive spirit for the causes of peace, love, and justice in the world. Some do. Most don't. In most Christian quarters, subversion is the enemy. Consequently, there remains an uneasy gap between the Way of Jesus and the way most American Christians live out our lives.

We live within sight of the day, just a few years from this writing, when the majority of Americans will be unaffiliated with any church. The era of the Christian society has now ended in the United States. Watch how quickly the moral majority politicos, as they increasingly fail in their attempts to force their values upon the larger society, are shifting now to a narrative of religious freedom for the minority! The shift from offense to defense for the Religious Right offers a noisy little sideshow to the more pressing narrative of Christianity's social marginalization.

Citizenship no longer means Christian. The church is no longer the center of life. Organized religion, in its Christendom edition, is growing more and more irrelevant and we are at a loss as to what to do about it.

But, we should add, there's a new state church in town, quickly rising in its influence. It is not evangelical. It is not Muslim. It is global, and it is formidable.

You see, even as the old forms of religion diminish, the empire continues to expand through globalization in every aspect of life: economically, politically, culturally, and psychologically. In some respects, this is good news that leads to expanding markets, more networks of connections, awareness of the plurality of beliefs and cultural expressions, and the capacities to work on global issues such as world hunger and climate change. It is a postmodern playground that emphasizes choice, diversity, and shared knowledge.

But it is also news that should raise concern. Left unchecked by the social justice conscience of faith communities (Christian or otherwise), this empire will likely continue to consolidate power and wealth in the hands of fewer and fewer corporations and people. What appears to be more choice is actually a commodification of beliefs, worldviews, and cultural products.

Authors Brian Walsh and Sylvia Keesmaat in their book *Colossians Remixed: Subverting the Empire* write, "What is at stake in globalization is not only the production and consumption of products but, more important, the construction of a homogenized global consumerist consciousness. Globalism wants more than your pocketbook, it wants your soul."[12]

Walsh and Keesmaat continue, "Globalization isn't just an aggressive stage in the history of capitalism. It is a religious movement of previously unheard-of proportions. Progress is its underlying myth, unlimited economic growth its foundational faith, the shopping mall its place of worship, consumerism its overriding image . . . and global dominion its ultimate goal."[13]

This becomes especially precarious in our postmodern world when there is no unifying meta-narrative to check this kind of greed. Instead we find ourselves like fish swimming in the waters of unrestrained consumerism driven by unethical capitalism.

However, one of the most subversive texts in history is the Bible. The Christian Scriptures came together during that time (well before Constantine) when the church was still a threat to the status quo. They build upon the prophetic traditions in the latter portion of the Hebrew Scriptures. The Hebrew and Christian Scriptures repeatedly and invariably legitimize the people on the bottom, and not the people on the top. The rejected son, the barren woman, the sinner, the leper, or the outsider is always the one chosen of God! The combined ethical vision of the Hebrew prophets and Jesus offers a vision of life that remains the gold standard for championing social justice. It is readily embraced by nearly all religions, and by people of no particular religion.

Does the church still have a story to tell the nations?

In the words of Isaiah 6:8, "Whom shall I send? Who will go for us?" To which we mumble: "Lord how can we go for you when we are in decline and fearing for our own institutional survival? Lord how can we go for you when we have co-opted the empire's gospel of scarcity fearing that we will never have enough?"

What would it look like for the church to reclaim Christ's subversive gospel of abundance and trust that the kingdom of God is at hand? As the church moves into an unquestioned minority status, it's possible that we might get our old-time mojo back. Christianity was not born to be Constantine's lap dog, to play chaplain to power. It was born to shake the foundations of empire, to speak prophetically to power.

A growing number of people, both laity and clergy, are embracing the end of Christendom as a gift to the Jesus movement. We see this especially among church planters. These folks are more focused on helping to bring about the kingdom on earth as it is in heaven than saving the institutional church, Christendom edition. With this simple and elegant shift, much of what the current configuration of church struggles with is no longer relevant for these leaders and the people in their communities. Instead they are focused on discerning where the Spirit of God is already at work so that they can partner with this movement. Their compelling question is how can I be a co-creator with God in this neighborhood? How can we conspire together? Oftentimes that creation looks like rebellion to the church authorities—or just plain weird.

The Spirit continues to surprise even declining churches that have become disconnected with their neighbors, irrelevant to the unaffiliated, and diminishing through death. This happened at a tall steeple church in Washington state when the staff found out that three weeks before Christmas the majority of kids in the school across the street were getting evicted from a low-income housing project. Instead of living out of empire scarcity, the church rallied and raised $40,000 in a week to help those children. News outlets broadcast the story and people started showing up at the church saying that they wanted to be a part of a church that lives out this kind of kingdom witness. Even the owner of the housing project, feeling convicted, called the pastor, and they negotiated a way to keep people in their apartments for two more months.

In a complex, information-rich, fast-changing world it is easy to become overwhelmed, apathetic, and disengaged. But leaders in tune with the Spirit are finding a simplicity on the other side of this complexity as they honor the dignity of each human being and faithfully hold out hope for that unfolding realm of shalom. They persist in the belief that something better is possible. Subversion can be as simple as taking that next faithful step. This begins with a practice of deep listening with hearts attuned to God and then acting on that discernment. Sometimes the actions seem crazy—like Phillip going to the deserted road to await a random chariot and engage in conversation with an outsider or raising $40,000 in a week. In effect, these leaders have reclaimed subversion as an integral part of faithful living.

They are coming to understand that discipleship involves the practice of finding beauty in imperfection. It calls for the courage to live authentically: to awaken to the deepest level of our own life, to connect inner life with outer work, to reflect with action, and to experience inner transformation alongside the pursuit of social change. This can only happen when a community can bear witness to each other and to their neighborhood that the kingdom of God is at hand. It is a hope that is birthed out of humility. This process has very little to do with efficiency, financial sustainability, or strategic planning. Rather it begins with waiting on the Spirit and dancing with the *kairos* of God.

Kairos is a Greek word, used eighty-one times in the New Testament, that can roughly be translated as "the appointed time in the purpose of God." We experience *kairos* when ordinary time seems to stop and eternity shines through in utterly breathtaking and simple ways. There is an unlearning that seems to have to happen in the life of the church in order for us to have the eyes to see and the ears to hear the *kairos* of God. The difference is between pushing a boulder up a hill and riding a wave of grace. Much of ministry in the old paradigm is based on the ego of the leader and the organization to do good work, to grow, to accomplish and achieve. The dominant underlying motive is to prevent failure at all costs. The effort is staff led, volunteer intense, and time consuming. Dancing with the *kairos* of God, on the other hand, is letting go of the need to control the outcome. It is like stepping onto a dance floor trusting in the effortless, joy-filled movement of the Spirit of God to lead. Trusting that all things are possible replaces fear when we listen deeply for the movement of God and join in the dance. When we attune ourselves in this way, life becomes pure gift and sacrament—an outward sign of God's indwelling grace.

Subversion can be the simple act of giving witness to amazing grace. On June 19, 2015, two days after eight people were murdered in a racist attack at a Bible study at Emmanuel AME church in Charleston, South Carolina, the shooting survivors and relatives of five of the victims spoke to the gunman, directly, saying that they were "praying for his soul." One by one, they forgave him. This practice of love in community is steeped in a long struggle of hope for God's kingdom in the midst of the powers and principalities of an empire that has enabled slavery, oppression, racism, and greed. The saints of that faith-filled community of Mother Emmanuel proclaimed yet again that love is stronger than hate. This amazing grace spoke to power, and within four days global retailers Walmart, Amazon.com, Sears, and eBay all announced plans to stop selling merchandise with the Confederate flag. Numerous other organizations, including flag manufacturers, also joined the boycott. This grace provoked, at long last, one of the granddaughters of Jefferson Davis to tearfully implore her colleagues in the South Carolina House to bring down the Confederate flag at the South Carolina capitol building. It was this amazing grace that even the religiously unaffiliated proclaimed as people all over the United States sang along with President Obama at the funeral of Rev. Clementa C. Pinckney.

Christian subversion unites rather than divides. We see this with Pope Francis as he seeks to rise above the troubled institution that he leads, embodying subversion in his actions and encyclicals, and at the same time unifying divided peoples and nations. Francis seems to have discovered the communion of saints that exists beyond the bounds of the Roman Church. He has become a pastor to the world as he humbly eats with the homeless, heals the sick, and blesses the imprisoned. Simply by his graceful presence he has brought world leaders to their knees and raised issues of ultimate meaning and human worth to the forefront of world politics.

Subversive practices invite us to move beyond the doors of the church to actively bring about kingdom living for all God's creation. We do this first by living into the fullness of our own gifts. One of the most effective subversive questions to ask ourselves is "What are my gifts and passions and how can I use them fully as a co-creator with God?" Howard Thurman said it well: "Don't ask yourself what the world needs. Ask yourself what makes you come alive, and go do it. Because what the world needs are people who have come alive."[14] This "kingdom work" becomes a way of life as well as an invitation to follow Jesus. This means there is no clear boundary between work and life. The focus becomes using our gifts as a witness to the sacrament of life day in and day out. Even if that means working at a coffee shop, driving a bus, running a laundry mat, bartending, or living in a neomonastic community.

For us, the authors, much of our work relates to coaching and resourcing church planters. So many of them are showing up fully to this moment and to the places where they have been sent. It is an honor to stand alongside them. One church planter started driving a school bus so that he could get to know the people in his community better, much to the consternation of the hierarchy, who were upset that he was working two jobs. Another planter in New England sold his car and spent his first year biking everywhere so that he could get to know his community better. (We did not even know they made snow tires for bicycles!) He then proceeded to start a network of dinner parties that offer neighbors a taste of what heaven is about. Another was beaten and arrested by police during an Occupy demonstration as he stood as a witness for peace. Another moved into a refugee neighborhood in a large city and gave shape to a neomonastic community that invites the neighborhood to imagine and help bring about God's preferred future. Still another took his bartending gifts and heart for the homeless and created a Jesus movement beyond his wildest dreams.

Each of these courageous and innovative leaders received pushback from various places within the ecclesiastical hierarchy because what they are doing cannot be fully appreciated within a Christendom paradigm that is fixated on butts in seats and dollars back to the home office.

The institutional church scrambles all over the place looking for key metrics as it tries to conform to the economics of empire in an attempt to stem decline. Is it worship attendance, finances, program generation, or some other kind of participation? The ecclesiastical anxious ones move the goal line every couple years. And they seek to measure progress more anxiously even than public school administrators.

But consider the central phenomenon measured in the Book of Acts: How many people have decided to follow in the ways of Jesus the revolutionary? How many agents of transformation do we have? Though none come anywhere close to perfectly imitating Jesus, how many are making a serious attempt of investing significant personal resources of time, money, and energy in blessing their neighbors and toppling all that oppresses people?

To be followers of the Way of Jesus is to choose to alter the trajectory of our lives and to begin living by a set of countercultural values as epitomized in Jesus' life and teaching. It is to direct our lives toward the advancement of the kingdom of God. The focus moves from church growth to kingdom living in a movement so expansive with energy that not even the gates of hell will be able to keep it out.

The rise of Christianity within the communist societies of China and Southeast Asia in the last generation has been breathtaking. Christendom missionaries planted Christianity in China over a series of centuries, and, while it took root here and there, it failed to thrive. A Western-flavored church, something from another time and place, was alien. Furthermore, it was connected to cultural, economic, and political oppression from Western powers. It came with ridiculous baggage to say the least. And then, when the Chinese watched Christian Europe dissolve into a stupid and savage war in 1914, Chinese Christianity took a body blow. What is the worth of a religion whose followers fall to such depths of depravity and apocalyptic macabre? From this point onward, it was assumed that Christianity in Asia would be a marginal community of Europhiles and nothing more.

Then Mao Tse Tung, of all people, inadvertently handed Chinese Christianity a giant favor. In the late 1960s, during the Cultural Revolution, the authorities came for all the Christian preachers and hauled them away, never to be seen again in most cases. The Chinese government closed all the churches and assumed that this would essentially stamp out Christianity for good.

Almost no one foresaw what would happen next. A church without worship services and real estate and without clergy—such a church was beyond imagination for anyone who only knew Christianity in its Christendom forms. It was the ultimate plowing of the field. All the dead stalks and remnant of an old harvest was destroyed. Yet from that same field there came a church of 100 million people across the following four decades. It is unprecedented in all of history.

Once the churches were gone, the house churches appeared within months. They gathered secretly—to be caught meant that your children would be locked out of any chance for college and a good job. Over the years, they became less secret. As the numbers grew, people saw that the Christians were some of the best people in every neighborhood. Churches began to rent space. The gatherings got bigger. The government decided that they wanted no megachurches, so this forced the churches to divide and plant new every time a church hit one thousand people. Eventually, the government gave up its program of suppressing Christianity and began licensing churches, giving almost all of the confiscated real estate back. When Paul was in Shanghai for Easter 2011, the former Central Methodist Church on People's Square was a packed house. People kept getting up and leaving with more coming in. At first it seemed to be a community with intense attention deficit, but then it became clear—there were probably three times as many people who wanted a seat as there were seats, so that after half an hour of worship, many people would give their seats to the next people waiting in the stairwell. This went on through multiple services all day that Sunday. As of this writing, as long as they do not publicly criticize the government, churches are essentially free to do whatever they want, be they licensed or "underground."[15]

The Chinese church is all over the map theologically. Some of it is off-the-map crazy cult stuff. A lot is not. Much of it is surprisingly Western in paradigm as the value system moves from red suppression into blue and orange worldviews in the Spiral Dynamics model. The spiritual hunger is such and the movement is so massive that Beijing has given up seeking to root out churches that are related to ancient and orthodox Christian traditions. They do continue to seek to curb the growth of the stranger cults.

But perhaps the worst thing that could happen would be for the People's Republic to adopt Christianity as an officially sanctioned and state-sponsored religion—for that could be the beginning of an Eastern Christendom that would quickly water down the passion and depth of spiritual experience that enlivens the Eastern Christianity.

The Jesus movement, born out of subversion, is at its best when it is subversive.

4

FROM INSIDER TO ALL!

The Lord has redeemed all of us . . . all of us, not just Catholics.

Everyone! "Father, the atheists?" Even the atheists. Everyone!

We must meet one another doing good. "But I don't believe, Father,

I am an atheist!" But do good. We will meet one another there.

—POPE FRANCIS

When Beth arrived at one of her pastoral appointments she found the church locked down as tight as a drum, literally. Not only were the outside doors locked, but many of the doors on the inside were locked as well, and only a handful of people had the keys. This church considered itself open theologically. But when it came to actually getting in, a few people controlled all access.

In the new world, it isn't simply about who has the keys. There are no doors! It isn't about who believes the correct formula of things, who has the most politically correct website, who holds elected office, or whose family has been around since the Civil War. Church is fast becoming truly Open Space.[16] Country clubs and airline lounges can and will still play exclusivity games. But any church that tries to act as if they have something special that folks cannot get elsewhere deludes itself.

In the early 1990s, United Methodist bishop Heinrich Bolleter traveled to Romania for the first time after the fall of communism. He expected to find a faithless place. Almost every vestige of Christianity had been systematically obliterated over a time span of three generations. And yet he found people of faith. They were fuzzy on the doctrines, but they knew the heart of the Christian good news that there was a God of love who created them and cared deeply for them. Who told them this?[17]

There is a prophecy in the Book of Joel that the apostles sometimes referenced in their explanation of the Spirit's coming:

Then afterward
I will pour out my spirit on all flesh;
your sons and daughters shall prophesy,
your old men shall dream dreams,
and your young men shall see visions.
Even on the male and female slaves,
in those days, I will pour out my spirit.
Joel 2:28–29

Regardless of gender, age, social status, or sexual orientation, regardless of ethnicity or immigration status, regardless of church membership or ordination—and especially to the people deliberately locked out of power—the Spirit is available. The Spirit is on the loose. Showing up everywhere. Entirely out of control. The message is clear: no religious institution can expect to hold power over other people when the Spirit is equally accessible to all.

During the truly golden days of Christendom of course, the church colluded with the government in a grand attempt to hold power over the population. That run lasted many centuries.

Over the last four centuries, we shifted from a monolithic church organization to multiple (and sometimes competing) church organizations in most parts of the world. Yet, prior to the rise of the information age, it was still amazingly easy for our respective churches to propagandize us into believing that they held the keys to eternal life, that their preachers were smarter in terms of Bible mysteries, and that the sacraments were purer when administered by them. Even though we all grew up in a world where there were multiple churches, most of us still were led to believe that we were dependent upon institutional forms of church for our own well-being, now and in the hereafter.

Fly Delta or fly United, but don't go flying on your own!

Of course, now it is a new day. The Spirit has really messed things up for the Western organized religion industry. The scales have come off our children's eyes in an unprecedented way. We have even devout young Christians asking why exactly they should join a particular church as a member. And among those who are choosing to formally affiliate with a church, they hardly ever feel obligated to accept all of the church's doctrines literally. Church membership means almost nothing anymore—or it means only what each of us wishes for it to mean.

What difference finally does it make to the rising masses of young adults with green worldview whether the Baptist church ordains women or whether the Methodist church marginalizes gay people? Women and gay people have so many other options. All of us have multiple options! At any point in time, any of us can create our own church or create for ourselves a meaningful life without any church! Most people are done wasting time and energy in petty fights over church policies.

Of course, in an era of such rapid change and disorientation, there will remain a sizable minority of people who are ready to hand over a lot of trust to voices and institutions that help them find a sense of comfort and security. But across the board, we are about to witness a more precipitous drop in church membership for all groups in the Western world than anything we saw in the twentieth century.

Welcome to the world of the spiritual free agent! The drop in church participation is coming faster among the Anglo population to start. But all groups should see it between now and midcentury. I may be a person of deep faith in God. But if I am under the age of thirty, I cannot figure out what church membership has to do with my faith in God. And for many, this disconnect extends even to attending church functions and worship services. As one young friend living with a green-yellow worldview said to us, based upon her experience, "I see lots of churches, but I honestly cannot imagine why I would want to go to one."

It is hard to know exactly how much church participation will slide in the next thirty-five years, in part because we do not know how quickly new, nimble, and highly indigenous strains of Christian community will arise. As the population matures into yellow and turquoise worldviews, the possibilities emerge for serious spiritual awakening.

Let's imagine that by the year 2050 about one third of Americans are still involved to some degree in a church. Based on current trends, this is not unreasonable. Of that third, perhaps two in five would be church members. That would take us down to around 12 or 13 percent of the U.S. population! This remnant would choose, by joining a church, to live in an intentional covenant with Christian sisters and brothers much like their ancestors. They would think of themselves as members of Grace Church, and most of their spiritual practice and service would be related to Grace Church. Because this 12–13 percent, about *one in eight Americans*, are so deeply involved with Grace Church, they will quickly be able to see the value of the church's ministry and step up to the plate in helping to shoulder the financing of the ministry.

However, since the lion's share of funding for church organizations comes from members, such a drop in total church members in America spells the imminent collapse of many church organizations, simply for lack of funds.

Additionally, in this imagined world, just thirty-five years from now, there would be other key constituencies at Grace Church besides its members:

1. People who live in partial covenant—short of membership, they have some kind of defined relationship or commitment to the community at Grace. They are very likely participants in multiple faith communities on a limited basis in each case. They may go on retreats with the Grace church, do yoga at the Episcopal church, send their

kids to preschool at the nondenominational church, and worship half a dozen times a year at the church near the entrance to their subdivision—a church that hides its denominational affiliation (and they have never thought to ask).

2. Those who identify as Christian and who belong to no particular church organization. This extremely freelance group cobbles together their experiences and alliances, much the way that many of us work today, especially those of us who are writers. (There is no one to guard their orthodoxy but themselves.) Because these people are not strongly identified with a particular religious institution, they may sometimes be able to respond positively to a church's efforts in community work or in creating a ministry for their children, even though they do not sign on to the church's fine print. The fine print may matter little to people if they do not feel bound by it personally. This could partially explain why many secular people love Pope Francis for his style and symbolism, even though they may still disagree with him on many points of doctrine and social policy.[18]

3. Those who are open to Christian practice as part of a larger spiritual practice. These are trans-Christian, perhaps post-Christian. But they find the values of Jesus compelling. These folks may be as deeply engaged in spiritual growth as anybody at Grace. But they dabble in many traditions and are loyal to none. (Any kind of argument with these folks that Christ is exclusive will just strike them as a cheap power play by the management.)

4. Persons who fundamentally identify with a non-Christian faith tradition, but who are willing to play with Christians so long as the activity aligns with their core instincts and values. (A church planter in Boston who secured $60,000 in funding for a community children's ministry partnered with this category of folks.)

5. A vast legion of persons with orange, green, and yellow worldviews who have serious misgivings about organized Christianity are willing to partner with us very selectively and cautiously. They are happy to roll up their sleeves and work with almost anybody, even

Christians, on the front lines of blessing others, and even to go get a beer with the gang afterwards. But they will retain deep misgivings about organized religion, especially since the churched remnant will almost certainly be disproportionately blue and orange in their worldview compared to the total population. This persistent blueness in remnant high profile churches will continue to complicate attempts by church leaders to rebrand Christianity for people in the green, yellow, or turquoise zones.

By midcentury, almost every human being you know will be steeped in the habit and practice of modularity. In the book *Making Space for Millennials,* the Barna Organization uses the motion picture industry to illustrate modularity. On one hand, fifty years ago many movie actors were practically owned by the studio where they held their contracts. Today, they are almost all freelancing, utilizing an agent to negotiate their varied deals. In a modular world, we engage with our jobs, our church relationships, our political alliances, and our significant others in very customized terms. It's all on our terms. If our airline of choice disappoints us, we choose another airline. If our bank slaps a giant fee on our account, we are out the door, switching to another bank. If our church changes pastors, discontinues a program that we like, or makes a social statement we disagree with, we will choose if we shall stay, go, or adjust our participation level. We hold all the power.[19]

This trend represents an enormous challenge to the current models of sustainability for church organizations. Both of us love the ideal of tithing one's income to invest in the things of God. But we also recognize that the ways that rising generations of Americans relate to this principle is shifting. The case for tithing one's income to the church has historically been based on passages of the Hebrew Scripture that do not really envision anything like the Christian church as it came to exist in later centuries. While we believe the practice of giving away a tenth of our income to bless others and extend the kingdom is a beautiful life practice, it is not mandated in the New Testament. Furthermore, even if it were mandated, most millennials will not be arm-twisted by any random Bible verse to part with their money, scarce as it is compared to what their parents had at their age. Further, even if they were to find a percentage-of-income approach to giving to be a compelling practice, it would further strain their thinking to imagine why on earth any particular religious organization should be able to claim rights to all of their donation. Young tithers today famously spread the blessings around to many more causes and organizations than their grandparents did. And they give money at levels significantly less than what their parents and grandparents gave, even after adjusting for differences in church involvement.

We suspect that many of today's young adults will grow into very generous supporters of charitable endeavors, including churches. As people grow in their personal identification with the values and movement of Jesus, their propensity to give and sacrifice for the good of others inevitably increases. But few churches will be able to demonstrate full claim on the generosity of a free-agent generation!

To raise financial support in the future, churches will have to make a strong case for the positive world and community impact of their ministries. There will be very little automatic financial support based on membership or loyalty to the organization. Any church without either endowment or a seriously compelling case for its ministry will dry up and blow away.

Another implication relates to worship attendance. In recent years, active church participants in America attended fewer worship services than they used to. Basically, the three-weeks-a-month people have become two-weeks-a-month attendees, and so forth. This trend has established itself so quickly and so universally that it comes up in conversation in almost every church that we visit. In a world of reduced loyalty to single brands of churches, increased competition for our precious weekend time, and increased technological possibilities for accessing spiritual teaching online, we anticipate that the regularity of live worship attendance will continue to slide and that many churches will de-emphasize large-venue worship gatherings.

As equally good home options for spiritual engagement arise, people will likely choose convenience. Online options will be as basic to the twenty-first-century church as Sunday school was in the twentieth century.

Most churches may hold flesh-and-blood worship gatherings as well, but the people who show up at the church buildings will be a decided minority of total participants in many of the healthiest churches. And everyone, in flesh and online, will participate on their own terms, around their family's needs, at convenient times, and in conjunction with participation in other engaging ministries, charities, and hobbies.

The biggest danger that we see in this shift away from institutional loyalty is that some churches could seek to become even more consumer-oriented, simply as a matter of survival. Indeed, the "Spiritual Theme Park" church, discussed later in chapter 23, represents one of the most highly consumerist forms of congregation ever conceived. Already, orange value-meme leaders in some denominations have fixated on metrics and benchmarks in a manner that belies their rising anxiety that the company shore up its consumer market share. While we expect that the thriving churches in this century will be savvy about understanding the needs of constituents, most of the churches and spiritual movements that really take the lead in the twenty-first century will be profoundly more about the kingdom than about rallying funds and warm bodies for their own organizational survival.

One of the encouraging trends in twenty-first-century church life is the rapid rise of multiethnic congregations. We are seeing a steady shift from church as almost universally homogeneous in types of people to a mixed situation—some churches are becoming much more diverse, even as some retain homogeneity. The younger the people in a church and the higher their education level, the more likely we see diversity. A rising wave of smart young adults has no clue why churches should be so ethnically and culturally segregated. They live in a world of endless human variety. They are energized and entertained by this. They date and marry across ethnic and cultural lines that their parents would never have considered crossing. While certain ideological and lifestyle issues still provide powerful social barriers for them, ethnicity and even religious heritage are often no big deal.

Multiethnic churches are thus forming with greater ease—sometimes without any intentional design. The launch team doesn't have to necessarily fixate on diversity training nor must the pastor be in a mixed-race marriage, *if*, in fact, the team carries solid life experience and relational skills that come from time spent with multiethnic schools, athletic teams, circles of friends, and so forth. Increasing numbers of people are ready to enjoy a party, a club, a workplace, or even a church where people who look like themselves are a minority of the total, so long as they are taken seriously as human beings and treated fully as part of the gang, with all the opportunities for leadership that any other would have.

A new congregation in suburban Maryland discovered two years into its journey that it had no ethnic majority. Its denomination assumed it would be a mostly white church. But the community is made up of highly skilled workers from around the globe, and it just became something better.

It is a story unfolding in hundreds of places simultaneously.

In the twenty-first century, the answer to the Pharisees' classic question "Who is my neighbor?" is exactly what Jesus taught: All are neighbors. All are sisters. All are brothers. All are potential allies and collaborators for good in the neighborhood. For increasing numbers of Americans, the radical thing St. Paul said in his letter in Galatians—about there being no Jew or Gentile, no male or female, and so forth—is no longer radical. It is assumed.

Beyond the multiethnic church, we will soon witness the rise of the church that invites multiple faith heritages into a very simple alliance around the Way of Jesus. Already our churches are full of individuals who self-identify as both Catholic and "fill-in-the-blank" (Methodist, Baptist, etc.). In the not-too-distant future, it will be very common to see people in churches who consider themselves both Christian and "fill-in-the-blank." We will see churches that love the Way of Jesus and also give careful attention to the wisdom of Confucius or to a particular school of Buddhism or even to teachings from Islam. A decade ago Thich Nhat Hanh's book *Living Buddha, Living Christ* foreshadowed the possibilities of faith collaboration that lie before us. These collaborators would argue that once one internalizes the message of Jesus, the core idea of the kingdom of God, there is no threat from other religious traditions. Whether or not they are right, we will soon see.

In such a church open to all, the sacrament of baptism is not viewed as an orientation to a club of insiders, but simply as a sign of God's grace for that individual in her journey. Nor does following Jesus circumvent continued participation in other holy and helpful practices and communities from beyond the Christian traditions (any more than it prohibited participation in the Jewish synagogue in the early decades of Christianity). And the sacrament of communion is always a gift to any who desires to celebrate the life of Jesus that still pulses through human veins. These symbolic acts come into their fullness as they awaken us to the deepest level of our own life and ultimate meaning. Sacred rituals and symbols will grow more important as people move into green, yellow, and turquoise value memes.

It is hard to know what Mahatma Gandhi would do with the twenty-first-century church. But if one no longer needs to cease being Hindu in order to be Christian, our hunch is that he would discern a place of much fuller communion with the Christian community than was possible for anyone to imagine when he lived a century ago—and likewise we with him.

This may still strike many readers as borderline heresy. But we predict it will be a no-brainer for some of our children and most of our grandchildren in the latter half of this century. The doors have been blown off. And the sheep will come and go. As they will.

But we are not our children and grandchildren. And what may be easy for them, we may experience as difficult, even as sacrifice. Letting go of certain habits and practices of faith identity that functioned to separate us from the rest of humanity can be terribly difficult. Many of the real sacrifices that were required of New Testament characters related to leaving cherished faith community identity and insider status for the bigger world into which God was inviting them. St. Paul had to give up his tough-guy fundamentalist-like approach to faith in order to become a pastor to Gentiles. Peter's challenge may have been tougher still: he concluded he would need to give up Judaism altogether as his primary faith identity so that he could be a part of a more universal movement. This was huge. The early Christians were stretched in countless ways, but the most rigorous stretching was the kind that challenged all those grandfatherly talks on the Sabbath and at Passover, where they had been carefully formed to distrust people outside the tribe. The distrust and sense of boundaries were important parts of the development of Jewish religion in a pluralistic crossroads of the world. But there came a moment in their lives when following Jesus challenged them to move beyond a tight tribal approach to faith.

To follow Jesus into a new moment in history, unlike any the world has ever seen, will require some kind of sacrifice from us as well. Because we all cling to different things, the sacrifice will vary from one of us to the next. But the theme of letting go remains. We each will struggle to let go of certain practices, mindsets, doctrines, liturgy, and so forth that are holding us back from reconciliation with our neighbors and our sisters and brothers.

For one person, this may appear as clinging to familiar worship liturgy that makes no sense to the people in the neighborhood and that functions to keep those people at bay. For another, this may appear as clinging to certain theological assumptions that go back to our childhood, which may have made sense to us over the years but are not required to follow Jesus, and which function to keep others away. For another, this may appear as clinging to standards of community purity and cultural norms, rather than allowing people of different experiences and practices to come close to us, even as we retain a common focus on that which is arguably more important.

One last observation on this: for all the increasing diversity of people who are coming together in the weird churches of the twenty-first century —*diversity is not an organizing principle.* It is not a rallying cry. It may be a core value of a faith community, but it is never the point. When diversity becomes the point, churches often just unravel. Or in planting situations, they simply never catch fire to begin with. There has to be a common *something* that binds us together in our diversity—this will be as true in the future as it was in the past. That something will vary somewhat from church to church. But every group needs identity, something to hold onto: a mixture of shared experience, compelling story, art, and core commitments.

FROM HEAD TRIP TO HEART WARMED

We are created with a drive to self-transcend, to move beyond oneself
for the joy and blessing of others. It is all positive, an original blessing
instead of an original sin, sending us toward a cosmic hope. There is
something within us, which Christians call the Holy Spirit, that makes us
aware that we are here to co-create with God and make something beautiful
of the world. Like the Trinity, the perichoresis (divine dance) of God, we are
made to encircle others and creation in self-giving love, generosity, blessing,
and service. When you start positive, instead of with a problem, there
is a much greater likelihood you will move forward positively too.

—Richard Rohr

At the end of the twentieth century there were still many places in the United States where you could meet someone for the first time and politely ask, "What church do you attend?" And if they were between churches you could invite them to your home church. This was a socially acceptable way to be neighborly and hospitable. Fast forward less than two decades and this same question would be awkward and bordering on rude in many communities.

Every year so far into this new millennium, the number of Americans attending worship services each weekend has dropped. That trend will only accelerate as the baby boomers age out. During the past decade the number of adults who are unchurched has increased by more than 30 percent. This is an increase of 38 million individuals—that's more people than live in Canada or Australia.[20]

We can no longer assume that the people we meet go to church, have a Christian background, or are even interested in religion. There are now more flavors of faith in many communities than flavors of ice cream at Baskin Robbins. New age, agnostic, atheist, spiritual-but-not-religious, none-of-the-above, in addition to classic traditions such as Christianity, Hinduism, Buddhism, Judaism, and Islam. And within each of these traditional categories there are yet many more flavors and belief systems. A new generation of spiritual free agents feels at liberty to mix the best insights and practices from many traditions into their own personal practice. After all, if you can have two scoops, why make them both pistachio almond? No matter how hard we try, we can't go back to just vanilla and chocolate, Protestant and Catholic, pretending that the Christian church is the only religious or spiritual option in town.

Even though millions of Americans are leaving church practice, they, for the most part, continue to be interested in spirituality and heart-warming experiences of the Holy. More than half of the unchurched adults in America are actively seeking something better spiritually than they have experienced to date.[21]

Millions of people long for deep connection in a community of belonging. They look for rituals that will ground them in something beyond themselves.[22] They are interested in the practices that will help them to grow in the ways of love as well as make a positive difference in the world. They are looking for what unites rather than focusing on what might divide. They would resonate with John Wesley when he said to the Catholics in his midst, "If your heart is as mine, then let us join hands."

When many church leaders read this they think, "If they would only give my church a chance. We are all about this." But there is a marked difference between a third-person concept of God presented in most churches and a lived-out first-person experience of the Holy.

Most Western churches continue to pursue what Phyllis Tickle called a "believe, behave, belong" approach to church. We assume you are coming to us as a Christian believer (or at least with a history of some sort of Christian belief) and our job is to assimilate you into our church culture and hope that you will join our local franchise. Church membership, in this instance, is typically based on a person's assent to a set of propositional truths *about* God.

In some cases, the set of propositions about God is freshly abridged, updated, and concise—so generous theologically that almost any mammal could assent, if they were sober. But still it is fundamentally propositional. It may be really thoughtful theologically, but it's still a head trip. Many of the people who are still joining "believe, behave, belong" churches may look at the list of beliefs and mumble, "Whatever . . . The kids are happy in Sunday school. Where do I sign?" Not a lot of passion there.

It is important to understand the history of our Western cultural landscape in order to understand why the church so often focuses on propositions as the starting point of Christian identity. In the Age of Enlightenment, during the eighteenth and nineteenth centuries, cultural and intellectual forces in Western Europe emphasized reason, analysis, and individualism rather than the traditional lines of church authority. Science became the realm of the public, facts, and knowing, and religion was relegated to representing private faith, values, and subjective belief. This was manageable in a Christendom culture where the church still had tremendous market share and continued to be part of the imperialistic push for Western domination of the world. During this time we read of missionaries trying to "convert the savages" and make them into proper citizens of the colonial expansion. Those savages were lost and they needed to be found. With this ethnocentric view of the world, evangelism became a valiant hard sell for the souls of any who were not like us. "If you are not like us, there is something wrong with you. Your salvation lies in becoming like us. And if you don't, we will not include you in our vision of a safe and compassionate world."

The vast majority of missionaries over the last 250 years were saintly, sacrificial people—not the creepy guy of Barbara Kingsolver's much-read novel *The Poisonwood Bible*. A better image of missionary is Vincent Donovan in his autobiographical account of the conversion of the Masai people in East Africa, in his classic work *Christianity Rediscovered*. In the latter case, Donovan patiently worked to develop non-European metaphors for Christ so that the Bible made sense in a very ancient/traditional culture. Yet still, even Donavan presumed that the heart of the evangelistic enterprise was to find a belief foundation as the beginning of the spiritual journey. It was a nearly universal assumption within the Christendom church.

Across the Atlantic, as the United States entered the industrial era of the twentieth century, mainline Christianity often became a matter of civic participation: something that folks did on Sunday—our common "day off." In most mainline Protestant churches and in most of Catholicism, people went to church to learn moral values. They were united in viewing Jesus as one who leads humans to moral change. Church members learned right from wrong, good from evil, us from them. They sang hymns about the aspects of the Trinity and recited prayers to a distant Godhead. Some were told that if they prayed and went to church they could get to heaven. Others were told that if they accepted Jesus as their personal savior they could get to heaven. Most people still believed that their church had a God-ordained license to broker those kinds of salvation deals.

For most of the twentieth century, people could attend the same church, quibble about the nuances of their beliefs, and still take communion together. This is the nature of twentieth-century American civic organizations. When there were major disagreements, one could always go down the street and join a group that better aligned with one's beliefs. The variety of church (and belief) options on the western side of the Atlantic is one reason that American Christendom outlasted European Christendom by at least half a century.

For millions of people, to be a good Christian meant showing up on Sunday mornings for worship, volunteering for a committee, and giving financially to the church. Church membership offered an eternal life insurance policy for relatively reasonable premiums, with the added benefit of promoting good moral citizenry.

Historian Timothy George has documented how fundamentalist evangelicalism originated from a marketing scheme by the founder of Quaker Oats. Early evangelicalism was just too wild and unpredictable for the titans of American big business. They worried that the social justice teachings in the Bible might feed a Marxist uprising. So they cooked up a new form of Christianity, fixated almost entirely on personal behavior and submissiveness to Christ, strongly flavored by American patriotism. It made for a stable workforce, less likely to fight for better pay or working conditions. The rising American middle class swallowed this new theology hook, line, and sinker.[23]

Yet, please remember that for all of the centuries of Christendom (fourth century to twentieth) church institutions mirrored political institutions, focusing on rules, order, rewards, and punishments. It was a sixteen-hundred-year marriage of power and authority, a marriage that survived even the Protestant Reformation. It makes sense that a shame-based systematic theology thrived across those years.

This shame-based theology starts with the premise that we are fallen and need to be saved, due to Adam and Eve being kicked out of the Garden of Eden for disobeying God. Jesus' death was necessary as a "sacrifice" to appease a just God for the sins of humanity. Only a perfect and sinless "man-God" could pay the price for our sins and redeem humanity. *Without the death of Jesus on the cross we would not be saved from eternal damnation.* If people could not accept this truth, then there was little point to Jesus' earthly ministry or to the way of life that he modeled.

This theology, called substitutionary atonement, took off in the eleventh century with Anselm of Canterbury and then gained momentum five hundred years later with John Calvin during the Reformation.

"Do you believe that Christ died for your sins?" continues to be a dividing line between the believer and nonbeliever for many churches. The premise behind the question is that human beings are fundamentally unworthy creatures who need the saving power of Jesus' death on the cross to redeem their worth in the eyes of God.

This shame-based theology is rooted in the doctrine of original sin.[24] But not all Christians embrace that doctrine. Tony Jones writes, "The account of the original sin in Genesis 3 teaches us a lot about the state of human nature, our freedom to know right from wrong, and our proclivity not to trust God. But it does not teach that the sin of Adam and Eve is responsible for the sins of subsequent generations."[25] Jones goes further to outline the three different interpretations of the story of Adam and Eve. The Eastern Orthodox teach that we inherited death from Adam. Western Christians include guilt along with death. Reformed Calvinists see our inheritance as guilt and total depravity.[26]

Blood payment for guilt and total depravity made sense to medieval theologians operating out of a blue value system, and the idea has continued to make sense to people in blue value system communities up until the present day. But today these assumptions about God are problematic on many levels. Today many ask, through our orange lenses, "Why would God choose to save the world through the death of his Son if God can do whatever God wants? It just doesn't make sense." And through our green perspective we ask, "If God is love, what kind of a warped Love would kill his Son to appease his anger with all of humanity?"

In all fairness, many churches have now moved to a much less shame-oriented understanding of the Christian good news, aware that there are at least five different metaphors of atonement (becoming one with God) in the New Testament. Yet the loudest voices in our religious marketplace, and in many of the largest churches of our day, continue to perpetuate the notion of God as a primitive king whose honor must be restored with blood sacrifice. The voices of the latter continue to define Christianity in ways that offend many Christians, in addition to sensitive, thoughtful people outside the Christian faith community.

So millions of people every year simply move on. Move on, as in moving on past continued participation in any church. There are multiple reasons why Americans are leaving church. They are not exactly the same reasons that drove the exodus in other places decades ago. Some are leaving today because of their perception of Christianity's required theological propositions. Others are leaving over other issues. But once we are removed from the echo chamber, the core arguments of a shame-based theology begin to look more and more ridiculous.

Only a very tiny fraction of postmodern people will ever reattach themselves to any church that chooses simply to double-down on a shame-based theology, or to craftily repackage it. Yet the majority of today's growing churches continue to recycle yesterday's theological patterns. This may help to grow individual congregations as they scavenge the religious marketplace of a dwindling group of refugees from the ruins of Christendom—but it is not helping at all to turn the overall tide toward a renewed Christianity.

In our increasingly networked, multicultural world, faced with some really big problems like poverty, war, and the possibility of a climate collapse—people both inside and outside the church are wondering, "What are those Christians talking about? What is the church really saving people from? Aren't we all connected? And doesn't our continued existence on this planet require us to find ways to break down the barriers that keep us suspicious of each other?"

More than a few are thinking that the church is one of the main harbingers of an us-versus-them dichotomy. This is worse than mere irrelevancy. The church increasingly looks to millions of people more like a part of the problem than a part of the solution. Many postmoderns view the church as a primitive institution. They may use all sorts of words to describe it, but essentially they see the church as stuck in a blue, ethnocentric paradigm that causes more harm than good. They see the church advocating a way of thinking that promotes banishment, death, and destruction for those outside the tribe. In a recent study by the Public Religion Research Institute, more than 70 percent of people in the United States that claim no religious affiliation agree that religion causes more problems than it solves.[27]

It is interesting how the mainline churches have found themselves stuck in this modern/postmodern quagmire fighting among themselves for ultimate truth. In nearly every denomination, there has been one sector calling for a return to right belief with a strict moral code under the eye of a judgmental God as a way to navigate back to the era of Christendom. In nearly every denomination, others (often those shifting toward a green value system) have poured themselves into ministries of social justice. "We are good people and we do good things. You will know we are Christians by our love; just don't ask us about our theology."

We have tried to reclaim lost adherents by co-opting business models focused on metrics-driven strategic plans. We have tried to move from the private realm of morals to the public realm of business. To no avail. We find no evidence that the recent fixation on mission statements, core values, and sales/production goals has made an iota of difference in the overall downward trajectory of organized Christianity in North America.

In the more liberal churches, even as there has been a promising theological shift away from the shame-based theology, there has also been a rising anxiety of political correctness. People are sometimes frozen with the fear that they will offend someone by appearing morally judgmental. It is quite odd. As if to say, "We will watch your children after school for free. We will feed you and clothe you, but we wouldn't think of inviting you to know the love of God by inviting you to be a part of our church community."

The movement of the Spirit is always of the heart. The kingdom of God cannot be thought into reality. It is more than an intriguing idea: it must be passionately lived. And that passion does not stop short of imagining a full spiritual communion between the servants and the people served.

Churches that cultivate and encourage passion and heart have fared much better in recent years than those churches that have sought to keep things safe, highly managed, and cerebral. Experience is a big deal today. It is worth remembering that all the heady ideas that churches ever came up with grew from experience—experience of God, experience of reconciliation, experience of healing, experience of serving one's neighbor, and (of course) experience of transformation.

The spiritual-but-not religious (SBNR) crowd is on to all of this. In some cases, they see churches more accurately from outside than the church people can see from inside. Some of the SBNRs are connected to a worldview that is more holistic, connected, and spiritually grounded than anything they could imagine finding in a church. It isn't that they don't think there is some form of Higher Power or Holy Presence in the world. They simply no longer see a clear connection between good moral living and institutional religion—or even traditional theism. They sense that human beings have within themselves the basics of what is moral and good along with the values that are necessary to make the world a better place for all. Christians also have a term that accounts for this internal moral compass: *Imago Dei*.[28] They are not interested in diddling their time away in religious clubs; they are yearning for transformation, healing, wholeness, shalom. They want to be a part of the solution. They want their lives to matter.

John Wesley, the father of Methodism, was a child of the Age of Reason. He struggled with the question of faith. As he began his career as an Anglican priest he understood faith as *fides*—a rational assent to propositional truths. However, when he looked death in the face on a sailing ship caught in a violent Atlantic storm, he realized that his dogmatic faith shriveled in the corner while a group of Moravian Christians sat next to him in a state of peaceful prayer. He longed for that kind of faith. He was told by his Moravian mentor to preach faith until he got it. Then, as any good Methodist knows, it was during a Bible study on Epworth Street in London that John said he felt his heart strangely warmed and he experienced a different kind of faith—*fiducia*—a sure trust and confidence that *even he* was a beloved child of God—a personal experience of God's grace! It was only when his head (*fides*) and his heart (*fiducia*) were engaged together that the Methodist movement was born. It was as if Wesley found a new way to read the Bible and to look at the world, through the eyes of grace.

This sense of unmerited, unconditional love was so powerful in Wesley's life that he wanted everyone to experience it—the paupers, the drunks, the uneducated, the servants, women, children, and men in every social strata. He developed what Methodists came to call "the means of grace"—specific practices by which we can open our hearts to that sea of grace that is ever present all around us. It is through that heart warmed with abiding love that we discover our passion and claim our purpose. As with the disciples at Pentecost, these practices help attune our hearts to our spiritual selves and our connection with the Holy Spirit.

If we snatched John Wesley from the eighteenth century and plunked him down 250 years later, in the context where we find ourselves, there is no telling how he would react—what he would say—how he might adapt or retrench in horror. Fortunately for John Wesley, this test will not be required. He ran well his race. Everything that he did, everything that he wrote, was contextual to another time and place. But we are still wondering. How and where are postmodern hearts strangely warmed by the Spirit today? Is it not reasonable to imagine that the answer today might be just a little different than it was in eighteenth-century England?

There is another story that we rarely hear about in the West. In the earliest centuries after Jesus, tales about him and his followers traveled to Africa, Persia, India, China, and the Celtic strongholds of Britanny and Ireland as well as to the people who lived throughout the Middle East. These lineages include the Greek, Russian, and Coptic Orthodox churches, the Ethiopian church, the ancient Syriacs, the Nestorians, and the Malabar Christians.[29] These traditions are notable because they were not mediated by the Roman church, nor by Western dualistic sensibilities and presumptions about Jesus.

As the West focused on morality and sin, the East focused on divinity and death. Jesus shared in our suffering and death so that we can share in his divinity through the resurrection. In essence, our journey to God is dying to this life and waking up to God in us.

According to Cynthia Bourgeault in *The Wisdom Jesus*, there was no word for salvation in the language that Jesus spoke, Aramaic. To be saved was "to be made alive." In the Christianity of the East, Jesus was *Mahyana*, the Life-Giver, the Enlightened One. The focus was on the Way of Jesus, which was a path that we can follow to become enlightened as well. What Jesus did is something we are called to do in ourselves. He offers us a way forward through his life, death, and resurrection. Jesus came as a teacher and catalyst for the path of ultimate inner transformation. According to Bourgeault, if this is true, "the primary task of a Christian is not to believe theological premises . . . but to put on the mind of Christ" so that we can become radiant (transfigured) with the light and love of God.[30]

This archetypal way is a path of letting go. Everything that Jesus did points to letting go. The Apostle Paul writes of this process beautifully in Philippians 2:9–16. He uses the Greek word *kenosis*—"to let go" or "to empty oneself." God so loves the world that God takes the form of a human being in Jesus. Jesus so loves us that he empties himself on the cross and becomes

Spirit who co-creates with us and will never leave us. The Cappadocians called this *perichorsis*, which literally means "the dance around." God reveals God's innermost nature of love through a continuous round dance of self-emptying. Christ invites us to participate in this self-emptying wheel of love where the first will be last and the last will be first. He reminds us that our freedom is found in dying to our ego and coming into a unitive "at-one-ness" with the creator/creation. This is the transfiguration that Jesus invites us to experience in the seventeenth chapter of Matthew's Gospel.

Cynthia Bourgeault writes that this kenotic outpouring of divine love is "more than just a path, this is also a kind of sacred alchemy. As we practice in daily life, in our acts of compassion, kindness, and self-emptying, both at the level of our doing and even more at the level of our being, something is catalyzed. . . . Subtle qualities of divine love essential to the well being of the planet are released... and flow out into the world as miracle, healing, and hope."[31]

John writes in his Gospel, "In the beginning was the Word, and the Word was with God. . . . In him was life, and that life was the light of all people. . . . The Word became flesh and made his dwelling among us" (John 1:1–14). Instead of viewing the world and our humanity as lacking and depraved, we could join our religiously unaffiliated sisters and brothers to reclaim our belovedness, to claim the treasure that is within us. Our invitation could be to help people to awaken to the sacrament of life and invite them to the dance of love and light in the world. It moves us from a sense of "God is going to get you" to "we are all a part of God's good, whole, and beautiful creation"—from retributive justice to restorative justice. It is a movement from a religion beyond morality to a religion of actual transformation of consciousness.

Pierre Teihard de Chardin, a twentieth-century French philosopher and Jesuit priest, is said to have put it like this, "We are not human beings trying to have a spiritual experience; rather, we are spiritual beings having a human experience."[32] Everyone has a spiritual life because we are spiritual beings. We express it in many different ways: not only in places of worship but also in work, community, and family, in all our creativity and commitments. When we connect with and live out of our spiritual core each breath becomes pure gift and life becomes a series of unfolding miracles. Sacraments are no longer relegated to a prescribed list written in church doctrine but rather become an outward and visible sign of God's grace unfolding every moment in the world. Our role is simply to wake up to this grace and join in the dance.

Although the spiritual life may take many forms, it is first and foremost about love. Perhaps the most profound and pure experience of this love occurs in what the traditions refer to as contemplation. Brother Lawrence, the seventeenth-century Carmelite friar, called it "the loving gaze that finds God everywhere." Through these heart-opening contemplative practices we become more aware that we are a part of that divine dance.

We have a rich history of contemplative practices that include, but are not limited to, deep listening, centering prayer, lectio divina[33], serving our fellow human beings, pilgrimage, music and singing, sacred ritual, journaling, telling our stories, and labyrinth walking. Such practices move us from third-person worship to direct communion. They help us awaken to the sacrament of life. This presence of divine love in and with us is a dynamic, continually moving flow that seeks goodness, truth, beauty, peace, and justice.

A twenty-first-century population explosion of people in the yellow and turquoise worldviews are coming to an awareness that we can be both spiritual and religious. By midcentury, the current orange and green worldview aversion to religion may be significantly tempered by a rising openness to the truth and wisdom available to human beings from ancient religious sources. This may be the Pentecost-like game changer of our century.

Frederick Schleiermacher, whom many consider the father of modern Christian theology, said the following in his *Addresses on Religion* in 1799:

> Religion is the outcome neither of the fear of death, nor of the fear of God. It answers a deep need in man. It is neither a metaphysic, nor a morality, but above all and essentially an intuition and a feeling. . . . Dogmas are not, properly speaking, part of religion: rather it is that they are derived from it. Religion is the miracle of direct

relationship with the infinite; and dogmas are the reflection of this miracle. Similarly belief in God, and in personal immortality, are not necessarily a part of religion; one can conceive of a religion without God, and it would be pure contemplation of the universe; the desire for personal immortality seems rather to show a lack of religion, since religion assumes a desire to lose oneself in the infinite, rather than to preserve one's own finite self.[34]

The journey, as Schleiermacher intuits, is one of letting go of our ego's need to be in control and losing ourselves in the sense and taste of the Infinite. It embraces the truth that God is in all that is because everything that exists is held in existence with Christ-consciousness. When Jesus says in John 14:6, "I am the way, and the truth, and the life. No one comes to the Father except through me," he is inviting all of us to have an encounter with this life-force of grace that he lived and lifted up. It is the Way of the kingdom of God— the upside down reality where shalom and justice define all things. The invitation to trust in the power of the gifts of the Spirit—joy, love, peace, patience, kindness, forgiveness, and compassion—allows us to transcend all institutions and religious dogmas. We might not be able to agree fully on our beliefs, but we can certainly agree on the centrality of love.

That great anthem "Woodstock," written by Joni Mitchell during what many call the birth of the postmodern movement, epitomizes this new awakening. "I'm going to try an' get my soul free," she wrote. "We are stardust. We are golden. And we've got to get ourselves back to the garden."[35]

If your heart is as mine, then let us join hands.

FROM BROADCAST CONTROL
TO SOCIAL COLLABORATION

Media . . . the idea that professionals broadcast messages
to amateurs, is increasingly slipping away. In a world where media
is global, social, ubiquitous and cheap, in a world of media where
the former audience are now increasingly full participants, in that
world, media is less and less often about crafting a single message
to be consumed by individuals. It is more and more often a way of
creating an environment for convening and supporting groups.

—CLAY SHIRKY

W e are living through the largest increase in expressive capability in human history. The amount of new information released daily into the world as of 2015 is equivalent to a twenty-foot high shelf of books wrapped around the equator. By 2020 that shelf will be thirty feet high and exponentially growing! We create as much information in two days now as we did from the dawn of humanity through 2003. At the turn of this century we waved goodbye to the industrial age and entered into the information age. Eric Schmidt, CEO of Google, said at a technology conference a few years ago, "I spend most of my time assuming the world is not ready for the technology revolution that will be happening to them soon,"[36]

The newspaper industry certainly wasn't ready. Craigslist, a free classified-ad web-based service, decimated the classified advertising departments of many newspapers, some of which depended on classifieds for 70 percent of their revenue.[37] Quickly this disruptive innovation helped lead to the demise of the print newspaper industry. In his book *The Vanishing Newspaper,* Philip Meyer calculates that by 2043 newsprint will be dead in America. Meyer is probably conservative in this forecast.

Clay Shirky in his TED talk "How Social Media Can Make History" reflects upon our media revolutions. He says that the printing press, telegraph, and telephone enabled us to create conversations—one person communicating with another person. Recorded media like movies, radio, and TV allowed us a way to communicate to groups, one message to many people. The Internet, however, is the first media in history that supports groups and conversations all at once—many conversations and groups to many conversations and groups. The Internet has also become a site of coordination. Groups that see, hear, watch, or listen to something can now gather virtually and talk to each other as well. This means that the former media audience can also be the creators of media. Everyone, everywhere, at any time can share their stories. We just need to look to social media platforms such as Twitter, Facebook, YouTube, Instagram, and blog sites as examples.

Every revolution in media has been followed by revolutions in the church as well. Don't think for a minute that we are going to make it through this latest media revolution without an unprecedented corresponding revolution in the way we do faith community!

The Gutenberg printing press with moveable type was invented in the 1440s. In the years that passed from Gutenberg's era to Martin Luther's Reformation in 1517, the printing industry expanded and improved to the point where books became more affordable and people began learning how to read. Without the use of this technology Martin Luther could not have pulled off a revolution on the scale of the Reformation. The printing press was used for the publication of propaganda against the Catholic Church and also provided notices alerting people to debates and rallies. It was the medium that produced thousands of Luther's pamphlets, which were in turn distributed throughout Germany to France. More importantly, the printing press shifted people's consciousness toward a more democratic way of engaging in Christian practice.

This movement that began in Europe continued in the form of the Great Awakenings in the newly formed United States. These uniquely American movements advocated for the idea of individual salvation and free will instead of predestination. They greatly increased the number of Christians in both New England and across the frontier. It is interesting to note that the invention of the telegraph in 1851 and the telephone in 1861 marked the end of the Great Awakening movements as well as the use of Circuit Riders to spread Christianity to distant settlements of people.

The next great media revolution moved from "one-to-one" conversations to "one-to-many" broadcasts in the form of movies, radio, and TV from the 1920s to 1950s. By the 1960s most American homes had televisions that gave shape to how we see, experience, interpret, and express our world. It brought into our living rooms the civil rights movement, JFK's and MLK's assassinations, and the war in Vietnam. It dismantled the modern perspective of order and predictability, introducing us to the fluid and fragmented experiences of postmodernity. Woodstock, civil rights, feminism, sit-ins, and free love epitomize the beginning of the postmodern movement. The church mostly rejected this shift by recommitting itself to preserving the paradigm of absolute truth and an objective reality that it alone is privileged to define. However, it did take on the container of the broadcast medium with the rise of the professional pastor and megachurches.

It makes sense that the church as we know it today finds its comfort zone in a world shaped by movies, radio, and TV. It is not a far leap to think about a Sunday morning worship service as a professional broadcast news program with the preacher as the professional journalist. Just like a journalist, the pastor is schooled in a tradition and has learned the craft of communicating the truth. The professionally trained pastor almost unilaterally decides what message—from a reliable news source, the Bible—to broadcast to a congregation. The audience receives and trusts this message as much as they did Walter Cronkite, the CBS news anchor from the 1960s to the 1980s. (Cronkite always ended his broadcast with the line "And that's the way it is." And all the people sitting in their living rooms nodded, "Amen.") This is a one-way communication to the many. Likewise, the preacher as broadcaster hopes that the message will captivate and entertain the audience so that they will tune in again. In more recent adaptations, the broadcaster is more like Oprah than Cronkite, but still there is broadcast-management control over what shall be presented and taught.

The object with almost every broadcast model is to get butts in seats so that the pastor can communicate the truth to as many people as possible. Large worship spaces are essential, often in multiple locations, to maximize the one-to-many mode of communication. In this paradigm vitality is measured in terms of worship attendance (viewership), financial revenues, and volume of programs. The pastor, like Oprah, is often CEO, executive producer, and headliner personality. And the focus is on excellence in presentation and programming.

The new church-start model that works in this scenario is to start enough small groups that can eventually feed into and support the launch of a large Sunday morning gathering. The church planter strives to launch a new worship service with at least two hundred attendees in order to build enough financial capacity to support the infrastructure that produces the worship experience.[38] The music has to be good. In recent years, really good. In many ways, it is a show that is meant to captivate us and bring us back next week, and the week after that.

Walt Kallistad, pastor of Community Church of Joy in Phoenix, named this reality in his somewhat campy 1996 book *Entertainment Evangelism*. That book was not a critique but a sincere playbook on how to grow a megachurch. Kallistad was honest in naming and describing what his church did to gather a crowd. However, after he named it, the idea fell flat. People ran from the idea, as if they were ashamed. Yet, twenty years later, as we look at most seeker-friendly worship services, the entertainment motif is still primary, even if few people want to talk about it.

Broadcast church (aka the Sunday Show) is now a shrinking game in the United States. By midcentury, only a tiny elite of preachers will be good enough, or savvy enough in marketing and technology, to pull it off and attract followers—a very small number of highly gifted pastors with increasingly large audiences—and it will be increasingly Internet-focused.[39] (See chapter 23 on the Spiritual Theme Park church to see where entertainment evangelism is going.)

Just as the Internet and social media have disrupted the news industry—both paper and broadcast—they have also disrupted the church. An exploding social media universe of interaction has distracted and enticed hundreds of millions of people beyond the confines of being a regular viewer for any professional broadcast message. Ratings are falling across the board, whether you are Anderson Cooper or the President of the United States (who actually still delivers a weekly Saturday radio address—that virtually no one listens to).[40]

Social media gives people multiple platforms for sharing ideas, organizing movements, seeking support, asking questions, convening groups, making money, and watching the latest cat videos. We discovered in the Arab Spring that when anyone can be a reporter of the news as it is happening, movements can begin. Those movements can be as playful as a flash mob and as inspiring as regime change—messy for sure, but filled with Spirit! Social media empowers people to be full participants in the unfolding stories of their world. Now everyone has his or her own grasp of truth to share with multiple platforms to use. Some package it up rather nicely in ways that others find compelling.

There is no license, no ordination, no referee, and no traffic cop on earth able to control all the worldviews or parallel experiences of reality being shared in a given hour around the globe. It is enough to drive a medieval archbishop crazy! Anybody with a little style and something to say can become a YouTube sensation. Postmodernity has taken hold in the form of contextualized truth.

In this digital age many people increasingly wonder about the relevancy of the old broadcast model church. Why give money to support the overhead of the church when you can organize a meet-up group in a park or coffee shop on your schedule? Why sit through a sermon when you can listen to an inspiring TED talk while taking a walk or sitting on your back patio? Why drive in traffic to a meeting when you can create a Google hangout with friends from all over the world in your pajamas? Why watch a movie in a theater when you can access it on your TV at home?

It is time to expand our working assumptions about church and look to the creative ways the newspapers have survived in our social media world. But even more than that, we need to look at digital media platforms as a new way to re-imagine communities of faithful practice.

The few newspapers that are thriving today have adapted, innovated, and transformed. And they have only just begun. The *New York Times* created an idea lab and slowly began testing ways to gain audience and ad revenue online. In 2006 they launched a mobile website. In 2007 they began experimenting with driving readers to their site through Twitter. In 2010 the Times began to hire bloggers, who drove 20 percent more people to their site. In 2012 they published an interactive story-telling experience using many media formats. In 2014 they launched NYTnow, which is a mobile app with customized ads. In late 2015 they launched a virtual reality platform that will transform the way we experience stories. They are now requiring their journalists to participate in digital boot camps in order to keep up with how to use and navigate media trends.[41]

Adapting, innovating, and transforming have been key words that the institutional church has used when addressing the decline in people and money. But talk is only as good as the paper it is printed on. Instead of managing the decline, as many out-of-print newspapers chose to do, the church could decide to create funded idea labs, engage in transformative scenario planning, and support weird church innovation.

One key to the church becoming relevant again is releasing its death grip on the broadcast church model. Newspapers have discovered that the typical adult uses four different technologies to access news every week—online, print, mobile, and social media. They have found that all of their digital circulations are growing exponentially. Yet the church continues to invest in the broadcast/print model as the only game in town.

This is not simply about creating a great website with video media, blogs, and links to Instagram and Twitter in order to entice people to church on Sunday morning for a broadcast production. Rather, it is about reconfiguring church as a platform for creating environments for convening and supporting groups that want to grow spiritually and learn more about Jesus both virtually and in real time.

Google collects data from all over the world and then sorts it into useable bits of information for whatever questions you have. It connects you through its vast network to books, articles, people, and videos. It also connects you through Google+ to your family, friends, colleagues, and acquaintances beyond six degrees of separation. It does not require you to look, act, or believe a certain way in order to engage.

Imagine the church acting as a search engine for spirituality. Imagine the church viewing its ministry as connecting people through vast networks as it conspires with others for the unfolding of God's realm in the world even beyond the boundaries of Christianity. Imagine the church as a virtual network of the body of Christ where vitality is measured in terms of the transformation of the scattered community. Helping people to awaken to the sacrament of life through different formats could become the new expression of worship. Again this approach embraces ultimate truth—easily discoverable and accessible for a variety of people across many social-political perspectives—that the kingdom of God is at hand, within, and right now. Do you not see it?

Some untapped resources for Christianity could include YouTube and Vine.[42] No one that we know has yet entered this realm as a subversive personality for the gospel. There are a host of people in the mainstream who would listen to someone with integrity who invites us into their real world, warts and all. People are looking for mentors who struggle and make mistakes in real time but who also practice love, reconciliation, and kindness and occasionally speak truth to power in no-nonsense ways. They need someone who is able to speak of things that nobody talks of, like a good comedian who pushes the conversation to places we don't ordinarily go. They need to see themselves in these personalities and then be shown the ways of love, healing, and redemption. Generation Y Not is one such media sensation that is inspiring millenials worldwide via Facebook and YouTube with a message of hope, common humanity, and love.

The Christian community knows the importance of connecting with others. We understand that the values of love, kindness, reconciliation, and forgiveness can spread through communities, making the whole greater than the sum of its parts. We believe that the benefits of a connected life outweigh the costs. However, we haven't been able to understand how vast, elaborate, and complex our connections really are. The Internet could help us expand our horizons beyond the folks who show up on Sunday morning.

Christ sends people out, empowered to share revolutionary news of God's love. Imagine bringing that witness to the power of the worldwide network. This means collaborating and co-creating with nonprofits in our communities as well as people of other faith traditions. It means embracing the gifts of the nonchurchgoers, treating them not only as consumers but also as producers/beloved children of God. It means getting rid of doctrinal barriers in order to become an open-sourced, grace-filled platform for further creativity in spiritual practice. It means letting go of the outcomes as we listen deeply to the people we meet where we live and work.

Imagine everyday life and spiritual formation as an integrated whole. Imagine networks of people who learn from and empower each other. Imagine small groups of people getting together to dream about God's preferred future for them and their neighborhoods and then daring to make that a reality. Imagine an open-source movement where people are allowed to contribute as much or as little as they like. Image a potluck of sorts where everyone is fed spiritually and physically no matter what they bring to the table.

In our world of overwhelming data and information, each of us needs to find our own internal compass, our source of deep wisdom, our sense of footing in ultimate truth so that we can be rooted in something deeper and more substantial than what the digital world can give.

The role of the church in a free market of spiritual seekers set loose in unregulated conversation and collaboration is to engage in the interactions at every level, from the world political stage to the kitchen table. Instead of broadcasting our truth, maybe we could just set a table of grace.

The Apostle Paul, near the end of his life, reflecting from prison on his life's ministry adventure, writes, "We have had our conversation in the world" (1 Cor. 1:12 KJV). Paul adds that he has engaged this conversation with simplicity, authenticity, and by God's grace. He underlines that he never sought to cleverly package anything. Though he was blessed with a colorful personality, he was anything but an entertainer. And to this end, we suspect he would be deeply disturbed by the performer/audience routine that characterizes Sunday worship in many churches today.

Paul did occasionally preach sermons to large assemblies. The Mars Hill sermon in Athens comes to mind—and it did not go particularly well. Paul was at his best one on one and in smaller interactions. He did his best work in homes, in marketplace encounters, at the synagogue. Though some of his letters were later elevated to Scripture, Paul had no idea that this was coming when he wrote those letters. He was the very antithesis of a broadcaster. He was committed to a conversation—to a dialogue rather than a broadcast monologue. In this regard, his leadership is highly relevant to us as we figure out what Christian witness must become in the twenty-first century. Paul's example would suggest that the very best we can do is to engage well in the world's conversation on multiple levels and in millions of venues. Our task is to simply show up to the conversation, with humility and good humor, and to trust God's Spirit to bring forth the fruit from the interplay.

FROM CORPORATE OFFICERS
TO INCARNATIONAL LEADERS

We are all meant to be mothers of God. What good is it to me

if this eternal birth of the divine Son takes place unceasingly but

does not take place with myself? And what good is it to me if Mary

is full of grace if I am not also full of grace? What good is it to me

for the Creator to give birth to his Son if I do not also give birth to

him in my time and culture? This, then, is the fullness of time:

When the Son of God is begotten in us.

—Meister Eckhart, German mystic and philosopher, 1260–1328[43]

As we have referenced already, in the late stages of Christendom, the church became increasingly institutional. And we are not just talking overorganized. By institutional, we mean far more: that the church was intensely shaped (some would say warped) by the habits and proclivities of large organizational life in a colonial-expansionist age. Then you layer in the industrial revolution on top of that: efficiency, hierarchical management, mass production, franchising, and brand loyalty. Bake at 350 for a few decades, and the soufflé coming out of the oven is not anything Jesus would recognize. Or want to eat.

The modern history of corporate expansionism is not pretty. And with so few boundaries between church and culture in the Christendom era, Christians constantly found themselves tangled up in shady enterprises. And poor Jesus . . . he got kidnapped, and a few of his words twisted around to bless it all!

To kick off the modern era, the Roman Catholic Church, arguably one of the first truly multinational corporations, colluded with various European governments in their expansion, actually loading priests on the ships alongside the conquering soldiers. Then for more than two centuries, we had a gigantic Christian-sanctioned human trafficking economy, chasing down people like large game in Africa to ship them abroad as free labor. Alongside that atrocity, we saw the rise of the American churches, saturated with the spirit of manifest destiny, an American justification for political and cultural domination.[44] Then, by the late nineteenth century, large bureaucracy became almost an art form, both in the world of business and in government. By the early twentieth century in Germany, the Christendom collusion between church and expansionistic corporate culture careened off the road in the Nazi disaster, provoking decades of reflection and pushing German children beyond the orange worldview into green earlier than almost anywhere else.

But in the United States we never experienced such a wipeout. So we never reflected nearly as deeply on the way that faith and culture became so intertwined. German American ethicist H. Richard Neibuhr saw this as clearly as anyone, leading him to write *Christ and Culture* in the golden twilight days of Christendom, just after World War II.

As the Christendom era came to a close and church expansion waned, the corporate expansionist party mostly raged on without us. The Church Growth movement briefly put up a good fight to continue advancement of a corporate-expansionist Christianity, complete with CEO-style pastors.[45] But from almost the time this movement got started in the 1970s, American Christianity has been steadily hemorrhaging people.

Meanwhile, the "company" has mostly gone secular. Multinational private corporations and the United States government have continued to subvert human rights and local community resources to the interests of power and expansion. They always deny it publicly. Always. But it seems to be an endless dance. Even when Nike and Walmart resolve to run no sweatshops directly, they cannot control their suppliers. When Coke tells us that they are recycling and replenishing all the water they use, it sounds great, until we realize that there's funny math going on. For example, they take water from a well in India and replenish it in . . . Canada. Which means that wells and aquifers in drought-ravaged parts of India are still, in fact, not being replenished from the considerable water it takes for their factory to produce a bottle of product. This is typical, monotonously predictable, multinational corporate behavior, both in government and industry. And so as long as we live within a fundamentally orange worldview, it will be "world without end, Amen."

Behind virtually every multinational movement there seems to be violence, lurking in the shadows. Violence against workers. Violence against the environment and the earth. Violence against local cultures and communities. And quite often, the violence presents itself in an actual shooting war, invariably justified by noble values.

So, you might ask, now that churches are more marginalized from power than ever before in our lifetimes, what's the problem? Christians today are of one mind about the evil of slavery. No one finds it fashionable to evangelize at gunpoint anymore. More than half of the folks reading this opposed the Iraq War. Even though half of the shirts that we wear are made in sweatshops, we all are against sweatshops. Right? Some of us may be feeling particularly proud that our church has not served coffee in a Styrofoam cup in twenty years. (Although, if there is finally a last cup of coffee ever to be served in a Styrofoam cup, it will either be in a church fellowship hall or the waiting area of a tire store.)

The problems are two-fold: one, we are all still customers of the multinational enterprises, feeding them with our money, and many of us are also citizens of a nation that continues to function with the mentality of a multinational corporation. Many of us are employees of such enterprises.

The fact that the United States promotes human rights in many ways makes it easier for its government to justify continued expansionism and control of world affairs and our meddling in other people's business. When you hide behind high ideals, it is easier to get away with fighting sketchy and questionable wars. So this is one problem, that we all are still connected to this stuff, even if our church got thrown out of the poker game, and even if we don't go to church anymore.

But the more specific problem related to the future of the church is this: even though the church finds itself increasingly marginalized from the corporate expansionist culture, we still retain the org chart, the theological baggage, the hymns, the clergy certification bureaucracy, and even the bellicose, in-your-face facilities that were designed for an age of orange. We still try to function like the Company that we were.

And we yet wonder why our green-worldview children can't relate to the church?

What does it mean to practice our faith in a different sort of way, to lead in a different sort of way, to organize community in a different sort of way? What does it mean to shed the baggage that we accumulated during the years of our collusion with violent world domination? Folks, this is about more than creating a coffee area in the lobby and softening the landscape facing the street. It's about more than downsizing the board and moving to consensus-based decision making.

What does it mean to relearn how we do church so that it aligns more with Jesus and the New Testament? How can we multiply our impact on the world for good and for blessing, while minimizing our cultural (and carbon) footprints? In other words, how do we expand ministry without trampling on people and the beauty and wisdom that they bring to the table? How can we extend the upside-down kind of kingdom (the anti-kingdom) that Jesus taught and not just a religious version of the "kingdoms of this world"?

There is a multisite church in Detroit called Redford Aldersgate. It started when a dying church of mostly white people dared to embrace their diversifying neighborhood in one of the most socially and racially segregated cities in America. Over the last few years, Redford Aldersgate has become wonderfully multiethnic and multicultural, even though they still retain a white majority of members. They began to grow as healthy connections with the neighborhood occurred. So far so good!

Then the denominational leaders saw a struggling African American church a few miles away (Brightmoor) and asked the growing church to adopt it as a campus.

The typical practice these days with such takeovers is to mirror what corporations do. The new management brings the magical DNA, the stuff so good that even Snow White will wake up when she smells it, and the former members are asked to step aside. "Thank you for your service, but we can take it from here." If the church taking over is growing in its ministry, it almost always works. It works in business. It works at church. The customer base expands and revenues grow accordingly. The denomination gets its cut, and the bishop's office is funded for another season. What is not to love about the "adoption model" of church planting?

But in Detroit, when the majority white church took over ministry management of the majority black church, another dimension in the dynamics of takeover were revealed. These dynamics were revealed because of the very complex issues of race relations in America. But the issues transcended simply issues of race. Race turned the lights on to something bigger still: what Redford Aldersgate pastor Jeff Nelson calls "church colonialism." This is dangerous stuff related to the temptation to impose ourselves onto others, often because it feeds our own ego needs and quest for expanded power in the world.

Soon into the adoption of the Brightmoor Aldersgate campus, Pastor Nelson realized that the work would need to be far more collaborative with both the remnant church saints and with the neighborhood people than what he had first envisioned, or had read in the leading books on multisite ministry. The best asset, they discovered, was not the bigger church nor the denominational grant money, but rather the Holy Spirit and the people on the ground in the Brightmoor neighborhood. First order of business was to pray and establish trust on all fronts. Then, more praying, as the church discerned and discovered what emerged in the holy conversation. It slowed things down on the front end, but a wonderfully indigenous and hope-filled ministry is taking root, complete with a Free Store[46] and two very different worship experiences, one on Saturday and one on Sunday. It is in no way a franchise experience of the adopting congregation. And the emerging faith community seems closer to the spirit of the New Testament than the spirit of a Jim Collins business text.

In the United States, perhaps more than anywhere else on earth, large, expansionistic organizational thinking (with colonial ambition) saturates everything we do. It probably seeps into our dairy products and water supply. We eat it with our Cheerios and don't realize it. When you read Jesus' Great Commission (Matt. 28:14) in the American context, a different missional product often emerges than when that commission has been appropriated in other cultures. American church life has now so influenced the theology and missional thinking of younger churches in Asia and Africa that, even in these places, a certain distinctly American perspective continues to color many things ORANGE.

The shift from church leadership as a business enterprise to a spiritual enterprise is bathed in prayer, and deep, deep listening as a group of friends seek to discover what is possible with God. Once the God stuff becomes clear, you can find the help to write a reasonable business plan in a day.

We have struggled in terms of what to call the leader who emerges from prayerful discernment embedded in community. At first, "spiritual entrepreneur" seemed a nice counterbalance to "corporate officer"—because a key challenge for so many of us who lead in the church is to move beyond being Company schmucks for some human-designed organization to being meek and nimble risk takers ready to try new stuff with God. That would be more an entrepreneur. But then, we took pause. "Entrepreneur" is still a business term, with business baggage and no small amount of ego required—even if it is a term that we both love dearly. To simply frame this as a shift from Company loyalist to maverick entrepreneur—it's not enough shift!

We settled on the term "incarnational leader." Just as Jesus leapt from the holy womb into humanity and embodied divine love in human form, as leaders our life work is to give birth to Christ in real and tangible ways. This is exactly what happened at Pentecost when the hearts of the apostles were blown open and they began resonating with Christ consciousness like ripples of transformation to the ends of the earth.

Jesus reminds us that the most important work for us to do is to make our home in God. Jesus says, abide in me as I abide in the Father. Attach to me and learn the ways of love. And when you learn these ways, share them with others. Love your neighbors, give shape to this world so that God's love not only breaks through but also is an ever-present kingdom reality. After all, you are love incarnate.

When we make our home in God we are able to let go of our lives lived in fear because we know that God is in us and guiding us in the midst of all of the chaos, conflict, and complexity that life throws our way. We can say "yes" to our life of freedom in God, a joy-filled life that produces on the outside what the Spirit has given us within. This enables us to live with integrity from the core of our gospel identity. We are able to lead with a sense of urgency that helps us to boldly try new things and fail along the way. We become humble agents with God, co-creating God's preferred future filled with a sense of fullness, wonder, and awe. We might not know the final outcome but we have a compelling vision and intuitively know that next faithful step if we take the time to listen deeply.

Before Jesus died he wanted his disciples to transcend the role of servant and embrace the way of friendship. "Love one another the way I have loved you. This is the very best way to love. Put your life on the line for your friends. You are my friends when you do the things I command you. I'm no longer calling you servants because servants don't understand what their master is thinking and planning. No, I've named you friends because I've let you in on everything" (John 15:12–15 MSG).

We are talking about the recovery of the pastor's fundamental role as spiritual friend rather than CEO or cocky sage-on-stage with gelled hair. This may not be an easy journey because it takes the pastor off the Lone Ranger savior pedestal and into the messiness of life where there are no easy answers or sure-to-succeed formulas. As a spiritual friend we may have more questions than answers and need more help from our communities to discern the way forward than a clear plan for success. Transparency in our thoughts and actions as well as having the capacity to be uncomfortable and vulnerable in the midst of ministry is important. However, this does not mean that we become a doormat or a self-deprecating fool for Christ. Rather, we humbly open ourselves to God's grace so we can be partners with the Spirit's unfolding in the world. The ability to set the table of grace and collaborate with others is key to being a spiritual friend. There is a sense of groundedness and gentle authority with this kind of incarnational leadership that resonates deeply in our souls. Dietrich Bonhoeffer, Dorothy Day, Mahatma Gandhi, and Nelson Mandela are examples of this kind of leadership that continues to inspire us to live out of our best selves for the shalom of the world.[47]

We believe that an unequivocal shift back toward the incarnational presence of the pastoral leader will do wonders in slowly healing the very bad reputation that Christianity currently has for billions of people. When you ask young adults from Chile to Canada, from Korea to Germany what they think about the Christian church, their answers are bracing—and increasingly similar in many developed countries. These are stereotypes disproportionately based on what people see on TV in terms of televangelists and media reports. Expect these perceptions to grow more widespread and provoke deeper anger as untold millions of folks move into the green worldview.

1. It is judgmental. The research by the Barna and Pew organizations have consistently found this to be the number-one criticism of organized Christianity among younger Americans.

2. It's a racket, a big business, and one that collects an awful lot of money for all the good it really does in the world.

3. It is just as often in the wrong as in the right, too often defending the policies and regimes that perpetrate injustice rather than working as part of the solution. (The church is lagging behind the population figuring out LGBT rights, and we would expect it also will be very late realizing that the climate crisis is real and a moral issue of the first order.)

4. It is boring: that is, spending a lot of time on matters that seem relatively irrelevant to daily life as we live it.

5. And churches that are not boring are still mostly about worship services, where it's talk, talk, talk, without ever getting around to really doing something to help people.

These perceptions about the church will not be easily dislodged. It is easy to see the footprints of corporate expansionist religion all over the place. A hard shift toward an incarnational paradigm will help immensely. But even then, it is going to be many years before the broken trust can be healed. Even if we radically renew church, the fact is that millions of people have seen something called church, and they have rejected it. It will take very careful work to communicate that we are not that which they rejected. Expect more than a few twenty-first-century faith communities to give up trying to redeem the c-word at all.

It is almost cliché now how many new churches create a tagline that says something to this effect: "A new kind of church." Or "Hate organized religion? So do we." Or "A church for people who dislike church." And so forth. Usually when we take a close look at the websites of such churches, there is little really fresh about them except that perhaps the pastor wears flip-flops, the band rocks, and they can drink coffee during the service (in Styrofoam cups half the time). Most such churches are just savvy tactical variations on "church-as-we-have-known-it." They are not weird churches. They attract mostly people with personal Christian history.

It is dangerous to generalize in such a dynamic age, because increasingly we are about to see some churches that break the mold. But up until now, the majority of the new expressions of church in America are still pretty conventional:

- Belief precedes true belonging, and the beliefs tend toward high biblical literalism.

- The pastor plays the expert, whether *he* is or not.

- The major program is a worship service for adults and simultaneous children's ministry—with an entertainment/indoctrination approach to both.

- They want contact information on us so as to develop us into regular customers and financial donors.

- Women are usually conspicuously absent from leadership and LGBT people are invisible entirely.

Both of us have coached people trying to plant this church. A few still hit the jackpot, typically when they have a large market of southern or midwestern suburban-Republican and/or heartland young adults who were raised in evangelical traditions and who are now raising small children. But it gets harder every year. The production-excellence necessary goes ever higher, and the fail rate also inches steadily upward. This church is not disappearing yet, not by a long shot. But it is going to become less common. The people who pull it off in the days ahead will typically begin with a pretty good core of folks from another church and, usually, with very nice funding. It is extremely hard to plant this church from scratch anymore—even though quite a few people were still doing exactly that just a decade ago.

But imagine a church that does not think of itself primarily in terms of a worship gathering or performance. It worships, but in simpler ways, perhaps smaller ways, perhaps gathering in larger number only monthly. Imagine a church that does not have a staff of seminary-trained pastors, and where most are bivocational. Imagine a church where there are multiple ways to belong and participate—no single paradigm of "membership," and certainly no expectation that a member do all of their serving and learning under this church's ministry umbrella. Imagine a church where at least half the gatherings are online, with participants often spanning the globe. Imagine a church where the people truly grab control. Where anyone can connect to the power and authority of the Apostles and baptize, wash feet, or serve bread and cup. Anyone. Imagine a church where there is a dynamic mix of faith traditions and ways of understanding God accepted within a single spiritual village, none diminished or threatened by the other. Imagine a church unified by spiritual practice, by love of neighbor and love of God, as best we understand each. Imagine a church that exists to develop children into world-changing leaders, free to create their own forms and spiritual alliances. Well, it would all be very weird, based on our experience. Imagine a church with a variety of mystical contemplative experiences, ranging from that which borders on Pentecostal to that which is similar to a Quaker meeting.

Some might say that it sounds like a new twist on Unitarian Universalist. But look again, and you might be very surprised. Animated and unified by a fresh vision of Jesus, it would be anything but a Unitarian church. It would, however, be weird.

"Who will pay for it?" some of you are asking. You ask this because you cannot yet see past the church as a cash-for-services business. There are unending business models for faith community. But there are also ways to gather and connect with one another that take very little cash at all.

"As denominational controls weaken, how will it guard against heresy and every crazy manner of beliefs and ideas?" some of you are asking. As if any church really controls what its people are thinking and what websites they are reading 24/7. Whatever is holy and nonnegotiable—any group can state this plainly. This is true in all times and places. After we state it, it's the honor system and the Holy Spirit. Maybe a more open source church will find better connection to the best spiritual traditions.

"How will it not just unravel and dissipate without a strong central organization and charismatic pastoral leader?" some of you are asking. Who is to say it lacks a charismatic leader? A spiritual friend is very attractive. And there are other organizing principles beyond an electric leader that may give gravitational pull to disparate people with varying agendas. A fresh vision of Jesus and a relevant and simple vision of what it means to serve our neighbors in the spirit of Jesus could hit the streets with such compelling relevance that we don't need highly charismatic leaders. Think early American Methodism where very average Joes and Janes animated an amazing movement that lasted over a century before it began to diminish in energy.

Fundamentally, it is all about renewing a simple faith in God. It is about relaxing our stance as leaders—depending more on God, and less on the shrewdness of our tactics. A lot more praying and a lot less long-range planning! It is about a shift from asking God's blessing on our big ideas to showing up to the places where we perceive God is working; and then picking up a dustpan and a broom, and maybe a Bible, and assisting. It is less talking and more listening.

Church leaders—this thing we are trying to build and develop—what is it anyway? Whose is it? We are so much more than church growth technicians sent by dispatcher to Church X. We, and all the people in our parish, are servants of the Risen Christ. We are agents of the kingdom *of God*, not *of ourselves*. It is not about us. It is not about our worship pageants and budget receipts. Sometimes our organizational efforts will thrive, other times not. Some experiments will succeed, and others fail. Some buildings will close and others will open. But if it is of God, if we are prayerfully and humbly aligned with the movement of Spirit in the world—do we think that this can be a failing enterprise?

Almost all human beings feel a need to prove our worth, and demonstrate our competency in whatever field we work. Especially true if we collect a paycheck for it. This includes pastors. We want to be good at what we do. But simply being good at what we do is clearly not going to turn the tide of Christianity's current decline in the West. Being brilliant at what we do—still won't do it. So why not give our "need" to God, and make the biggest paradigm shift that the realm of God invites. "Not my will, but yours." "Not my glory, but God's."

To summarize it in one of Jesus' best lines: "Seek first the kingdom of God, and all these other things will be added unto you" (Matt. 6:33 KJV).

SECUNDUS MOTUS

Glimpses of the Rising Church

THE SHORT CHAPTERS IN THIS SECTION represent snapshots into the future. We are getting far enough into the liminal sea that land is beginning to peek through the fog on the far horizon. The post-Christendom church is not all mystery—there is emerging clarity about what is coming, and with every passing year it will be getting clearer.

We offer these glimpses in order to capture the range and rich diversity of the twenty-first-century church. It is not a unified future! There are many futures before us. And our list is far from complete—just a few snapshots. Any time that we become passionate about a particular model or ministry paradigm it is easy to exclaim, "This is the future!" While this may be true on one hand, it is also always false. The Apostle Paul in 1 Corinthians 12:6 tells us, "There are different kinds of working, but in all of them and in everyone it is the same God at work." The same God, we would pray, also for the diversity of paradigms for church that will thrive side by side in the years ahead!

Some of these snapshots are decidedly weirder than others. Some only faintly exist currently—so that they stretch our imagination. Others are simply adaptations of ministry trends already well established. Some exist firmly within the "pay to play" monetized culture of the late twentieth-century American church, with very high financial overhead. Others are much less cash dependent, offering hope for groups with less income and/or less propensity to quickly donate income to organized religion. Some of these embrace all of the shifts we have just encouraged in the first half of this book and will discover rich partnerships with persons moving into green, yellow, and even turquoise worldviews. Others embrace only some of these shifts. A few are focused on the remnant of people in blue and orange worldviews and, as such, may not embrace many of the shifts at all. It is not as if the whole world will be living with green and yellow worldviews in the year 2050! Far from it! Beautiful and amazing human beings will live across a wide color scheme of value memes—and live faithful lives authentically within their framework.[48]

We debated the order in which to present these nineteen snapshots. The first nine are truly weird by the standards and sensibilities of highly organized religion—they seem lighter, generally simpler, and more organic. The next eight are adaptations of current more institutionalized forms. These eight range all over the color spectrum of Spiral Dynamics. The final two are special, one extremely common and the other extremely rare, each critical to understanding the rising twenty-first-century church.

In all cases, the churches unfolding and imagined in these pages are signs of the coming reign of God. Kingdom places! They reveal powerful things, biblical things, about the world God desires to bring to life! They are communities hosted and choreographed by people of remarkable Christian faith—and yet most of them stretch our understandings of membership in a faith community, in many cases collaborating with atheists, Buddhists, and loads of people who don't do such labels. Traditional Bible study may not happen in every setting, but it is hard to imagine any of these places where the conversation could not segue at any moment to a consideration of what the gospel of Jesus means for almost any question of human life.

Please note: the possibilities for online and virtual community exist within each of the snapshots. Having competency in social media and web interactivity is as basic as competency in children's ministry and sharing of Holy Communion in this century. We chose not to present virtual church as a separate snapshot because it will be a fundamental component of almost every imaginable scenario by midcentury.

Most of the churches that are designed for yesterday will vanish like the dinosaurs, and possibly more quickly than we currently expect. One particular type of church that will be nearly extinct by midcentury is the denominationally based, neighborhood franchise church waiting to get its box of curriculum and offering envelopes from headquarters. That church is about to disappear. Many of the center-city denominational flagships have already disappeared in the last years—a few have retooled and survived. Increasingly, the crisis is now moving to suburban contexts. These denominational franchise churches, with a weak local vision and identity apart from an old tribal brand, represent a staggering percentage of congregations across North America.

If that is your church, then we are talking in this book about *the end of church as you know it*! Now is the time for serious rethinking or for making your arrangements so that your spiritual and material assets can be passed on to others who will dare to partner with the neighbors and God to create a weird, new thing.

But before we start making out wills, lets take a breath and consider the possibilities in the pages ahead. Maybe one or two or three of them will help to stir longing and imagination within your church's people and kick-start you on the next phase of your journey together with God.

THE NEIGHBORHOOD

WE START BY MAKING CONNECTIONS. I do this by showing up at school, being on the PTA, volunteering at the Portland Art Museum, shopping at local businesses, serving on nonprofit boards, doing intake at a clinic for folks on the margins, and maintaining an active social media presence. All of this allows me to meet new people and build relationships. Others in our community do this work in a variety of ways. We are intentional about making space in our lives to form relationships with others and to be looking for new ways to connect and therefore learn about our communities. Most importantly, networking allows us to live love in lots of ways with a wide range of people. Most of the folks we network with never become part of our church, yet the ways we get to be present and share light and life are rich and part of the gift of this way of being church.

After we build relationships and connections we begin to see people who might be interested in some spiritual exploration. We invite them into a night at a bar talking about theology, or a hike in the woods with moments of meditation and reflection, or a worship experience based on silence and chanting, or a conversation about a book, or a project serving our neighbors. These are ways that folks can begin to experience this community and grow spiritually. People show up who are interested and we have a great time exploring faith and spirit together. The ability to meet people where they are and offer safe spaces to grow spiritually is amazing. This is the holy gift we give to our city. Of the folks who come to these events, some really are seeking a community to be part of and so we then invite them to dinner.

Dinner is the heart of our community. It's where we build deep, supportive relationships with one another. It's where we are renewed to go and do our ministries out in the world. Being committed doesn't mean coming every week, but it does mean wanting to be part of community and be willing to listen and love one another. This work is slow, and it is beautiful. It is holy and hard. And I could not imagine any better investment of our life energy, time, and resources.

—Rev. Eilidh Lowery, Sellwood Faith Community, Portland, Oregon

Churches grow from the rich soil of neighborhood. They are not like hydroponic tomatoes. They need soil. They need to put down roots within the latticework of relationships and communal identities that we call neighborhood. However, sometimes, after fifty years, all the church members have moved away from the streets surrounding the building and commute back on Sunday mornings from some other place. Such churches seem to be rooted in thin air. It is no coincidence that they are often experiencing system failure on multiple fronts.

Sandy Boone and her husband wanted to live on their sailboat and also plant a faith community in the varied marinas of Baltimore harbor, among the hundreds of people who have eschewed land life to live on boats. In the early days of planting a church called Water's Edge, she casually commented to Paul, "We came here to plant a church, but it quickly became apparent that we would first need to plant a neighborhood." So she began with activities that would help neighbors to come out from their highly isolated and atomized existence to meet one another. Birthday parties, book clubs, little mission projects to help others. One woman who had lived in one of the marinas for ten years said to her, "Oh my God, before you came, I didn't know anybody. Now we are the boat-hood."

Boone wove together a neighborhood of varied collaborations and relationships, and once she had several dozen people in that orbit, there were a half dozen ready to sit down and seriously explore Christian faith, in what Mike Breen calls a huddle. Over the years, some of the huddles evolved to house churches, and Water's Edge began to seriously reshape the social and spiritual waterfront of Baltimore.

Matthew Johnson is a church planter in partnership with a church across the street from the campus of West Virginia University in Morgantown. The new church is called Ignite. He discovered that the majority of the students and others that were in Ignite's relational orbit were not ready or interested in a weekly small group. So Johnson adapted the model that Boone used, even as he was planting a decidedly more conventional kind of church. By Ignite's second year, Matthew Johnson had deployed shepherds to tend to four different informal tribes of people: (1) undergrad students, (2) grad students and young adults who were remaining in the area post-degree, (3) residents of nearby housing developments, and (4) LGBT folks—who discovered that Ignite was the only church on campus that would be nice to them. In fact, each of these virtual neighborhoods became fertile soil for the launching of huddles, study groups, mission teams, and more.

In both cases, savvy twenty-first-century pastors have demonstrated that you can't easily grow a church without the soil of a neighborhood. They have worked the soil and even fortified it, apart from the planting of their varied religious gatherings.

In other cases, pastors and other leaders may discern that a rich and functional neighborhood already exists around the church, often predating the church. In these cases, smart leaders will simply get out in the community and tap in to the circles of good faith and good people that have already formed. Why start another food pantry when there already is one?

Why start a ministry to at-risk kids without collaborating with the Boys and Girls Clubs who already know half the children you wish to serve? Why throw a block party when there already is a well-established block party pulling together diverse people into a single community experience?

Better to find a creative way to join the party that is already happening and contribute toward making it even better! One church in Boston was asked to join in with an outreach effort sponsored by the regional Community of Churches. However, since most of those churches are so inwardly focused, the lion's share of volunteers came from that one community-minded church. It was a win for the ecumenical event (and those relationships), for the neighborhood, and for the community-minded church that saved itself the additional work of throwing its own party. Win-win-win.

The Neighborhood is not a church per se. But it is the universal platform from which churches emerge (both weird and conventional), and without which they cannot thrive. In some cases, we might call a Neighborhood a faith community, due to faith-oriented activity that happens here and there within the overall relational field. For the purposes of this conversation, we only designate something as a church when people sit down together and make a covenant with one another, moving toward a sense of intentional we-ness, focused upon loving God and serving neighbors. Such covenant communities almost inevitably meet the Vatican II definition of church as a sign of the coming reign of God.

In terms of church planting and revitalization, little good is going to happen apart from heavy investment in neighborhoods. In the years ahead, if the market of church-shoppers continues to dry up, it will become more critical than ever to plant Neighborhoods where links are weak and invest in Neighborhoods where promising links already exist.

This approach is a present-day expression of Jesus' instructions to his disciples in Luke 10 (which we explored back in chapter 2): take no preconceived programs, meet people, get to know them, eat with them, and discover the kingdom of God together. This takes time, and it requires deep exegetical listening. We must develop our ability to be the interpretive bridge between the sacred and the secular. In other words, it takes great community-organizing skills. The emphasis is on the priestly function of helping people to discover signs of God's presence and then inviting them into the fullest expression of that reality as community. For skeptical post-modern, spiritual-but-not-religious people, religious services are of little interest. However, community-building gatherings with an emphasis on making a difference in the world are often highly compelling.

Many excellent projects labeled "new church plants" these days are really in a pre–church plant stage, where significant neighborhood cultivation must first happen. Some of these projects are judged as church-planting failures quite unfairly, in that the leaders are still doing the foundation work requisite to a thriving church plant. For this reason finding pastoral leadership indigenous to the community and/or encouraging bivocational pastors will be key to helping these promising Neighborhoods to develop and thrive. Clarity about the assignment and the likely timetable of neighborhood development will help us avoid a premature conclusion that we can't plant churches in certain places.

THE SIMPLE CELL

I REALLY WASN'T SURE what I was getting into. My friend invited me over to her house church one Thursday evening and I met a bunch of people who intrigued me. I wouldn't call myself a Christian per se, but I am interested in growing spiritually. I have now been back about every other Thursday for six months. I have found a safe place to ask questions about all the things that I find offensive about religion. And I have discovered a community of acceptance that helps me to let go of my shame demons. I can share anything with our little house church.

We do all kinds of things together, like watching movies and talking about them, cooking meals together, gardening for our local food pantry, and serving meals at the local shelter. Last month, one of our best times was when we gathered on the lakeshore at sunset and read poetry. Each of us takes turns sharing our gifts and interests, leading, and hosting. I like how we read the Bible. They call it lectio divina. I am not exactly sure what the term means, but it invites me to listen to my intuition and to the wisdom of the group.[49] There is no pastor preaching a bunch of church baloney and no one tells anyone else how they should live. Instead we are on a journey together and I like that.

I am growing in ways I never dreamed possible and have not only expanded my circle of friends but have begun figuring out my "calling" in the big picture of life. It seems now my life—the good, the bad, and the ugly—is starting to make sense. This group is helping me to trust that the arc of my life is bending toward a good place. I can even say "God" now without getting twisted up in knots.

O*ikos* is a Greek word used in the early church to refer to "households" or "extended families." In the book of Acts, everything was based at the level of the *oikos*. One example is when Peter went to Caesarea and baptized an entire extended family who, in turn, became a Gentile mission outpost for the Jesus movement. This simple *oikos* configuration allowed the Christians to thrive in the midst of persecution and hardship for hundreds of years. In the last century, hundreds of millions of people have lived in contexts of hostility toward organized religion in which *oikos* gatherings again flourished. The *oikos* is the simplest form of church. But it is more than just a small group—it has all the DNA and core functions of a church.

Simple Cell churches are highly contextual and often function as an extended family. They may be organizationally connected to a larger movement, or they may pop up independently. They may be fundamentalist in theology or quite the opposite—they can be whatever the context dictates. In a time of emerging green and yellow worldviews, count on many cells to act much less sectarian than they would in a world of blue and orange. For the purposes of our *Weird Church* conversation, we are thinking about cells that relate intentionally to the Christian traditions.

Some *oikos* groups gather weekly over a meal; others meet a couple times a month. The groups typically gather around eight to twenty people on any given evening, with an orbit of people roughly twice the typical size of the gathering. People come when they can. It is a fluid configuration.

Leadership may be shared among the group or there may be a few key leaders who help to organize the gatherings, while others think about food, and still others think about organizing for community service endeavors. Connecting to each other, to God, and to the larger community is part of the covenant that is adapted to fit the movement of the cells as they grow in trust and spiritual depth. These cells can experiment with different ways of being together and may morph in the process toward almost any other form of church. Some cells are gatherings of families with children while other cells can be other flavors, such as widowed women, people going through transitions, stay-at-home dads, or young adults. Any flavor or tribe of people can become the *oikos*.

These groups configure, design, and direct themselves; everyone contributes and everyone is supported. The convener is the one who holds the space for safety and security so that people's souls can come out and play. If allowed, these groups naturally form their own practices and rituals, which may include lighting a candle, praying a certain prayer, singing a group song, or observing a certain way of sharing their stories and listening to each other. Their monthly rhythms often include worship, fellowship, learning, and mission.

The *oikos* could be as simple as a single-family household. Brett Wells and his wife, Rachel, in Fort Worth, Texas, have developed a simple family ritual with their young boys. They begin the day together saying, "Today I will pay attention, see Jesus, be Jesus, and mess up." They follow that with praying the Lord's prayer together before going off to school. When they gather around the dinner table in the evening their conversation is about what they paid attention to and how they saw Jesus, were Jesus, and messed up. As they began to wrestle with the real life situations that they brought to the dinner table conversations, they decided to add these phrases to their morning ritual, "I can choose my attitude. I can look for an opportunity, and we can find a way forward together." What a simple and delightful way to shape and form children to be followers of Jesus! This is the *oikos*—the lived-out practice of being a family in mission.

Linda Brewster, a nurse practitioner and part-time pastor to a traditional church in Portland, Maine, calls her Simple Cells G.R.A.C.E. Groups (based on the first letters of the gifts of the spirit found in Galatians 5:22–24—gratitude, reverence, acceptance, compassion, exuberance). She began two groups with people who are allergic to church—one meeting at night with adults and the other during the day with moms and young children. These groups have evolved in depth and connection as well as morphed to accommodate changing schedules and group size. One created a community garden and partnered with an existing church to create a monthly intergenerational VBS-like experience for families. They are small enough to be highly adaptable, simple enough to require little oversight or formal funding, and powerful enough that whole families are choosing to be baptized.

Zacc's House, a network of Simple Cells, began in Portland, Oregon, with Beth and five others who committed to grow spiritually together and launch house churches. The model is loosely based on John Wesley's bands, classes, and societies. The "band" is the group of leaders who gather to learn, discern, and grow spiritually together so that they can launch the house churches. The classes are the house churches that the leaders facilitate, and societies are the monthly gatherings of the classes that engage together in service work. Each house church creates its own rhythms and rituals as they covenant to connect to each other, to God, and to the larger community.

Mike Breen, when he was the rector at St. Thomas' Church in Sheffield, England, led his people to *be the church* instead of just going to church. A decade later Breen, along with a group from his church, moved to the United States and began to share the tools they had developed to help people be formed in the ways of Jesus. They gathered groups of people in covenant communities called huddles and then trained them to listen and respond to the voice of God, eventually passing along what they were learning by forming their own huddles. What has ensued is a movement called 3DM that trains people in this process and now extends around the globe. The gift of the 3DM movement is that it multiplies huddle groups by multiplying leaders in those huddles—disciples making disciples who make disciples, and so on.

Simple Cells are a logical next step for existing churches that want to extend their mission into the community of nones and dones (people whose religious preference is none-of-the-above and those who are done with church as they know it.). First United Methodist Church of Williamsport, Pennsylvania, is creating a network of microcommunities that will function together as an extension of First Church, but with measured autonomy. They are inviting a few of their members to step into their neighborhoods to help start these *oikos* groups with their families, friends, and neighbors. Just as Peter went to Caesarea, some of the people in First Church are going into their own neighborhoods to meet people where they are, to connect them with others who are interested in the spiritual journey, and to form *oikos*.

And yet, most of the people in the worship services of Williamsport First Church will stay right where they are. If you are comfortable in the world of the worship-centered American church, you are less likely to be attracted to a Simple Cell. And most American church members, even if they were to try to form such cells, would become overwhelmed at the thought of inviting friends and neighbors who are not church people, or who are not Christian. If there is one thing that most American church attendees are really uncomfortable doing, it is inviting someone to a church gathering. And the more intimate the gathering, the more awkward it gets.

So, unless a church is formed with a high value for *oikos*, most of its people will avoid such gatherings. Just as most postmodern people will religiously avoid worship services at the building with the steeple.

Different tastes for different folks! But as the attendance in the buildings with the tall steeples steadily declines, it is very possible that the *oikos* churches will buck the trend and grow in the years ahead.

IO

THE DINNER PARTY

WHEN OUR FRIENDS SAID they wanted to take us to church and out to dinner, we missed the detail that all of this was to happen simultaneously. We arrived at the church, noting that it was in terrible repair. "This is it?" "Yes," we were told. "Our church just rents space here from another church. The other church has only four old ladies left." I thought to myself, "I bet it's cheap rent." We went down the stairs—there was an old elevator, but it looked scary. Then we entered the basement and came upon a dingy world that had been transformed with Christmas lights strung all over the place, and candles lit on every table. The faint smell of musty basement was quickly overpowered by the robust and wonderful smell of good food. There were about forty people gathered, everyone so friendly, so relaxed. It was like . . . a good dinner party. Then came the Trader Joe wine bottles, and toasts to Jesus. Cheers. And the breaking of these magnificent loaves of bread—we were told to pull off a good-sized chunk as the loaf was passed—as it would be our dinner. A couple of guys had worked all afternoon in the kitchen preparing soup and bread. The soup was vegan, but as hearty as if it were loaded with beef. Every ingredient was fresh and local. There was enough to feed half the neighborhood.

As we ate, there was Bible reading, poetry, music, and people telling stories from their lives. It was all happening at once. We were not having a church service; rather, in a matter of minutes, we had simply become a church. Crazy. It was not clear who the pastor was at first—different people led different things. After they read one of the Bible passages, we paused quietly to reflect; then they asked us a question, but it was not some Bible expert kind of question, just a question about our lives. You could not stop the conversation. It was so interesting, so honest. I did not even know these people an hour earlier, and suddenly I was engaged in a conversation about faith in God, OF ALL THINGS, and I didn't even mind it. The pastor finally talked a bit—I guess it was a sermon. It was funny, and it was about life. When the evening came to a close, I thought it had been the shortest church service ever—but I looked at my watch to see that two hours had passed. My wife looked at me as we walked back up the stairs to leave and said, "We are totally coming back here again." Agreed.

Ask the leader of any Dinner Party church in the United States where they got this brilliant idea, and quite a few will cite a small church in Brooklyn with twenty people gathered on a typical night. A church with twenty people and a brilliant prototype of how church could be in thousands of places. The Brooklyn church is called Saint Lydia's. Saint Lydia's has not intentionally multiplied itself even once, never sent a group out to Queens as a daughter congregation, or anything like that. But their paradigm of church and the power of their liturgical experience have been so compelling, and so ridiculously easy to replicate, that they have inspired holy copycats, who continue to multiply Saint Lydias across North America, and soon, we would surmise, around the planet. As this paradigm multiplies virally in the years ahead, it is possible that few will remember the original Saint Lydia's, but people will still be expanding its impact and legacy. The Jesus movement works like this!

In some ways, there is nothing truly novel about a Dinner Party church. You will likely step closer to the experience of the primitive first-century church in a dinner party than you ever will in a more conventional modern worship service, modeled more after Greco-Roman theater than any early Christian gathering noted in the Book of Acts. In the context of a simple dinner party, you may gain a taste of the power and appeal of first-century Christianity that caused it to overtake the Roman Empire.

Even in communities with a highly secularized population and no small antipathy to organized religion, the Dinner Party church will often find its twenty to fifty people in just a few weeks. Of course, in the twenty-first century, there are infinite variations and cultural nuances from place to place. The theological flavor could range widely. But we would note that in a Dinner Party church gathering you are likely to get more Bible, more theological substance, more conversation, more relationship, and very possibly more ancient liturgy than you would ever find in most big-box megachurches, and to get it in a way that feels truly conversational and respectful of the diverse experiences and ideas in the room. For this reason, mainline Protestants are quickly becoming fans, as are their neighbors, who may have given up church attendance decades ago.

At one place, we heard parents talking about being able to attend church with their daughter and her kids, three generations in one place— like in the old days. But their daughter would never have attended a typical church. The dinner party format made possible something that had seemed beyond their dreams.

Root and Branch Church in Chicago is connected with the UCC and the Disciples of Christ. The night Paul attended their dinner gathering, he found himself seated across from a woman who was a judicatory overseer and next to another person who was not a church person at all. Yet, somehow, the setting served as an equalizer, where titles and roles did not come out early in the conversation, and people were able to engage one another simply as people: as friends on a journey together. The artful mix of good food, evocative music, and spiritual conversation made for an evening that would be hard not to love, even if church was not your thing. Even as the conversation became decidedly theological, the questions posed to the group were such that almost anyone would feel comfortable jumping in. (The wine did not hurt the process either.)

Simple Church, in Grafton, Massachusetts, is decidedly Methodist, so they pass on the wine and serve chilled filtered water instead. Simple Church has set a vision of intentional multiplication, quite different from the focus at Saint Lydia's. They are now taking on clergy interns and partnering with them to plant new Dinner Party congregations. Once the interns learn the ropes (and this is not hard to learn), they may choose to plant similar communities upon graduation. Simple Church is focused both on planting new congregations and on teaching existing congregations a new way of doing church—so that the latter can begin new services. In this way, Pastor Zach Kerzee sees possibilities for a proliferation of simple, low cost, indigenous faith communities spreading across New England—into all the places where the Methodists have been steadily turning out the lights for the last hundred years.

Tiffany Keith was inspired by The Moth Radio Hour when she began Stories@theEdge. Through her community organizing efforts she became friends with many people living at the edges of society in Colorado Springs. As she got to know their stories she discovered the power in listening to and sharing stories. She combines a dinner party atmosphere with three storytellers at each meal. Story guides help people to process and practice their story so they can feel comfortable sharing it during dinner. These guides actually become mentors in the process. After the stories are told the dinner guests are asked questions in a lectio divina fashion in order to reflect on how the story connects to their own lives. In this process of deep and prayer-filled listening they find themselves on holy ground—inspired, connected, transformed. Tiffany has developed teams of story guides, cooks, and dinner party hosts.

The brilliance of the dinner church model is that everyone needs to eat and most people enjoy dinner conversations. In overscheduled lives this gathering becomes a simple gift, filled with the best ingredients of grace. The food for these gatherings can be potluck, gourmet, takeout, or cooked together as a community effort. The importance is in the intentionality of the gathering, the rituals and the conversations. As often as we do this, we can remember Jesus' invitation to embrace the sacredness of life and our common humanity.

THE SOULFUL VILLAGE

I HAD ALWAYS BEEN A LITTLE CURIOUS about living intentionally with others, but I did not understand the transforming power of that kind of living until I became a part of this community. It started as a group of like-minded people, friends, who developed a covenant together for a shared life. All but one of them already lived in the Heights neighborhood; they met every day for prayer at someone's house, and once a week for dinner. As they got to know each other better, they began to look for a house that could accommodate all eight of them, with space for three or four more. They found this old mansion on Grand Avenue—it had been the mayor's house back in the day, but it had become really run down, and got chopped up into little apartments. They renovated it, doing much of the work themselves. They made that old place back into one home again, with seven bedrooms.

I live just down the street from that house: I have lived on Grand for almost thirty years. When I saw them hauling debris out the front door into a dumpster one day, I decided to make soup and serve them all lunch. I eventually started coming to their weekday morning prayer before work. I also now join them once a week as they open their dining room to all of the neighbors for a community meal. They still have one bedroom left available in that house. I am thinking of just having a yard sale, and moving in. Everyone who is a part of the community, whether we live there or not, agrees to give four hours a week to the needs of the neighborhood, as well as show up for morning prayer and the weekly meal. It is through these amazing new friends that the Heights got our first community garden and two huge neighborhood cleanup blitzes a year. At the last cleanup, we rallied eighty other people to pitch in. Our park has flowers again, for the first time that anyone can recall. We have also started a babysitting co-op for our working families and single moms. I have learned so much about the power of a village of caring people to advocate for a healthy and safe neighborhood. In so many ways, we are becoming the anchor of the Heights neighborhood.

Oh there are other churches in the Heights. Their people are very nice I am sure, but no one around here knows any of them. They drive from another part of town for a couple hours on Sunday and they leave. In more than three decades, I never met one person from any of those churches. Now I have a church, and even more—they have helped me to get to know lots of other neighbors. The Heights is becoming a new place. We are much stronger together than we ever were hiding behind our front doors.

The Soulful Village, like the Simple Cell and the Dinner Party, shares much in common with the early church. Some people call this "intentional community." Others have called the renaissance of this kind of church "new monasticism." In the Soulful Village a group of people make a covenant: a set of agreements that defines the nature of their life-sharing and the values of the community. Often the life envisioned in such a village captures the spirit of Acts 2:42–46, the classic passage that describes the life of the first Jerusalem church, albeit in an idealized manner.

The Soulful Village may involve persons living together 24/7 within a single residence or a small cluster of cottages or an apartment complex. It may also be a mixture of folks living together and those who covenant with them, but live nearby. In the twenty-first century, it will sometimes morph to a virtual village, experienced through advanced web streaming between like-minded souls positioned all around the world—perhaps linking individuals and shared life homes together across oceans and national borders. (The latter might be different enough to warrant its own unique category.)

Rev. John Schwiebert and his wife Pat with another couple formed the Peace House in Portland, Oregon, more than thirty years ago as an intentional community that shares resources, lives together, gathers every morning for prayer, and shares the evening meal. Both Pat and John were actively engaged in justice ministries and wanted to live out the early church practice of having all things in common. At any given time the house has four to twelve people living in community. Pat, a perinatal nurse, started a ministry called Grief Watch for parents who have lost their babies to early death. Grief Watch has become a cottage industry that supports the house through book sales and support groups.[50] Over the years hundreds of people have been trained in nonviolent justice practices as well as formed in values and practices of kingdom living as Peace House understands it. Many people in the neighborhood walk or bike to the house for morning prayer, as it has become an important way to start their day.

The Missional Wisdom Foundation, founded by Rev. Larry Duggins, an ex–bank executive, and Elaine Heath, a professor at Perkins School of Theology in Dallas, launched eight such intentional communities called Epworth Houses in Texas. Each house establishes a rule of life that shapes people in disciplined practices of prayer, radical hospitality, and justice. Each house develops in the context of its own neighborhood—they are not clones. Each house engages in hospitality with neighbors in a variety of ways, including shared meals, community gardens, and sustainable living.

Each Epworth House is connected to an anchor church in its local community as a way to mutually support one another in mission and service to the world. The anchor church is a conventional congregation, with a building and a Sunday worship service. Through their laboratory for

Missional Wisdom they are co-creating fresh expressions of Soulful Villages all over the United States that include co-working spaces, pilgrimage groups, and missional microchurches (each of which is reflected in other chapters of *Weird Church*). They seek out the places where people naturally gather and help them to see that God is in that place. (For more information go to missionalwisdom.com.)

We will see many more expressions of intentional living popping up all over the world as the green value system comes of age. Communal living, sharing resources, making a difference, and growing spiritually are a few of the reasons why millennials are reviving this monastic way of living. We also see this as an enticing way to create community, make a difference, and extend savings as more cash-strapped baby boomers retire. Some of these communities move into separate homes in a blighted neighborhood hoping to be a light of hope and leverage for change. Others transform large older homes into communal living spaces, and still others practice co-housing by moving into the same complex or tiny house villages in order to share tools, childcare, and weekly meals.

THE FAMILY CHAPEL

I LOVE OUR LITTLE CHURCH. The denomination tried to close us about ten years ago, but we are still around. I think we have eighteen people. We all know each other. And we care for each other. They tried to tell us we were not sustainable, that we needed to merge with another church. We could see no reason to do this. We have no debt and we have quite a hefty savings account to care for our building for years. We don't need anything from the denomination. We can take care of ourselves. We could even find ourselves a preacher, if they would just let us.

We don't want or need to be a big church. I mean, don't get me wrong: we would love to have some new people. We are quite friendly. Mary and her little daughter started coming just a couple years ago. But we do not want to get too big. Big churches are too much of a big business. And they start getting lots of different opinions on things, and have conflict. At our church, no one can remember us ever having a fight. We know how to get along with each other. We don't all agree on everything, but we enjoy the old songs and the fellowship—where people disagree, we don't press the issue.

Our preacher is not full time. She's a county court judge Monday through Friday. She experienced a call to ministry, but she already had a good job—and she doesn't really like big churches. So she preaches on weekends. We are just perfect for her. And I think she and her husband actually give back more than we pay her.

Did I tell you that we have a healthy little savings account? Mr. Jones kept our books for years, but he got too old. Now his son Kenny keeps the books. Kenny lives fifty miles from here, but he grew up in this church. He watches every penny, just like his dad. Just let them try and close us again. We are not going anywhere.

Indeed, the Family Chapel church is not going anywhere.

There are untold thousands of these small congregations across the United States. The majority of these churches are rural, often closing for lack of population. But there are so many of them to begin with, and they may exist in the city as easily as in the country. With so many churches shrinking in size, some larger churches may morph into Family Chapels.

Family Chapels are both denominationally affiliated and independent. They exist across a rather wide theological and cultural spectrum. They tend to gather in ethnic enclaves, but that could change in the years ahead.

Often denominational leaders have minimal respect for the Family Chapel. This type of church may not strongly identify with the denomination: often it sends little or no money to advance denominational priorities and structures; and it is too small to offer a job for career clergy. It is fair to say that there is little significant opportunity for denominational growth via the Family Chapel strategy.

But these churches are amazingly resilient, often hanging on for decades after the experts and ecclesiastics have written them off. Just when it looks as if they have too few people to continue, a couple of families who left another church in some sort of frustration will find them and join, putting a little church back in the game. Because they tend to be low-budget ventures, it doesn't take a lot to renew them.

The Family Chapel may keep a pastor for decades or change pastors every year or two. Because the pastor's main function is simply to lead the worship service, and because the essence of the church is the family-like relationships, the church may be minimally disrupted by short pastoral tenures. The church also may make most of its decisions without even consulting the pastor. The people may defer to a single matriarch or patriarch in decision-making. Or in some cases, where there are two, three, or four chieftains, they may simply establish consensus among themselves, and the rest of the church is almost certain to follow their lead.

The word "chapel" is operative in this type of church. In almost every case, the church is sentimentally tied to a quaint, historic building. The building may be much larger than the congregation that gathers—as these churches often had more people several generations back. But typically the building is not so large as to threaten the church with high maintenance expenses.

A century from now, after most of the current denominations have collapsed, merged, and faded, many of the tiniest congregations that they paid the least attention to will still be with us.

We should be clear that the Family Chapel is not cutting edge. Nor is it always a place of high hospitality toward outsiders. Nor is there strong evidence that it will grow significantly in terms of total participants in the days to come. But it is a durable institution, durable in part because of its simplicity and high degree of ownership among its member-participants. Because it values sociability and intimate kinship above doctrinal purity, it appears to be just as able to exist within a blue worldview as within a green. Time will tell on this. But the Family Chapel is anything but an endangered species in the twenty-first century.

THE COMMUNITY-BASED ENTERPRISE

WE STARTED BAKING BREAD, since we wanted really good bread for communion. Then we decided to bake extra and sell it in the neighborhood farmer's market. It was popular, so we bought special equipment so as to make and sell more. The baking is intensive, with thirty to forty loaves twice a week. We have different baking teams for Thursday baking and Saturday baking. But we price them at $12 a loaf, and people often give us $20. We made over $35,000 last year. This, alongside tithes and offerings from our church's core participants, made it possible for us to reach financial solvency with only about fifty persons a week in worship. Our presence in the farmer's market also gave us a reputation as (1) community minded, (2) down-to-earth, and (3) the church with the really great bread. We've made lots of new friends in the market. Some people give us prayer requests when they buy our bread and never show up at a worship service. About half our current group found us via the farmer's market. Next year, they are talking about giving our church the management of the whole market, which would further increase our revenues and the possibilities for positive community interaction. Our denominational leaders say that it takes 125 people to be able to pay a full-time pastor. They failed to consider that we might meet in a free space and do like the monks in the Middle Ages by creating a small business. We think we have changed the whole economic formula for how you do church. We are showing how smaller congregations can thrive.[51]

T he Community-based Enterprise is a strategy created by intentional faith communities many centuries ago in order to avoid having to beg or perpetually fund-raise. In a social and economic context where church taxes mostly went to established parish churches, innovative and upstart faith communities had to find a funding stream in order to exist. Especially if their members were withdrawing from the world to some degree in order to practice their faith, they had to find a way to pay the bills for the community. They came up with all manner of small businesses, much of it agricultural. This tradition has endured with many monastic orders until the present day. In every case, the work itself becomes a key part of the church's worship, fellowship, and service to the world. It offers value that transcends the revenues generated.

The Community-based Enterprise might involve food production, textiles, or marketable crafts. For a high-tech group, it could involve building websites for nonprofits and family business start-ups. In all cases, the work will generally run year-round and it will serve to shape the life of the faith community. For this reason, we often see a direct ministry focus and/or a strong metaphor of the church's mission implicit in the work. Occasionally, and rarely, it will grow into an enterprise that requires hiring workers.

Simple Church in central Massachusetts is developing a system where each worshiping community (its dinner churches) is integrally connected to at least one major enterprise. For one of the Simple Church communities, this is bread baking. For another, a small pumpkin farm could provide ample product for a major fall festival. In each case, proceeds from the business mix with donations to fund the ministry (which, we might add, has already been designed to have a minimal-cash approach). Pastor Zach Kerzee notes that this kind of ministry is a constant "hustle," keeping connected with people on one hand and starting up a small business enterprise on the other. There is both simplicity and intensity in the ministry design. It is not for low-energy leaders.[52]

One of the most common forms of Community-based Enterprise church is the coffee house church. We have marveled about what it is with young Christians and coffee—perhaps it is the nature of coffee as a community drink that is perceived by many to be more wholesome than alcohol. A megachurch in the Pacific Northwest shared with us a few years ago that they were closing their coffee shop because they could not make a profit with it. They remarked that the business consultant they used in trying to save the coffee shop noted that new coffee shops fail more often even than new churches—so it might be a questionable strategy to tie one to the other in a single enterprise. We advise our clients, unless they know the coffee business, to consider partnering with someone who does—who knows all the angles including the marketing. An excellent example of a church that did their homework and succeeded at this is Union Coffee Shop in Dallas, near the campus of Southern Methodist University, where Michael Baughman is founding pastor. Kevin Veitinger at the Foundry Savannah in Georgia sets his coffee shop apart with small-batch roasted coffee from a local roaster. Both Union and the Foundry Savannah use the coffee shop as a place where people can connect, form community, and collaborate in artistic, entrepreneurial, and socially minded ways to help bring about the shalom of the neighborhood. (Another variation on the coffee theme is Ebenezer's Coffeehouse near Union Station in Washington, D.C., a place with average coffee but a very nice vibe—although Ebenezer's is simply one ministry division of a rather conventional worship-driven multisite church in D.C. where the lion's share of finances comes from worship-participant donors.)

Membership in some sort of collective might come with a monthly fee or suggested donation (typical of shared work spaces). This might go beyond simply a way to help pay building costs, and it could become a major piece of a church's overall funding strategy.

Some churches are repurposing their buildings in ways that build community relationships and create cash flow. A preschool is perhaps the most common example. One very creative congregation located in a small southern German city a couple hours north of the Alps looked at their frumpy 1960s church building and figured out that the chances of getting their friends to walk into that place for religious services was a tall order. So they turned the church's sanctuary into a climbing center—and now have six hundred youth and young adults who are members of the center, paying an annual fee to practice mountain climbing the Matterhorn just a few blocks from their homes. Organizing weekend hiking and mountain climbing retreats in the high mountains with spiritual practice is the next step for them. Meanwhile, they hold weekly worship services in the banquet room of a popular local restaurant—and are drawing sixty or seventy people into an eclectic gathering with food, teaching, and worship—while they leverage the building they own to build relationships and nurture young people in life, and in faith to a certain degree. Running the climbing center seven days a week is a major volunteer commitment on the part of the church's members—but a commitment that they feel is worth it.

We wish to distinguish this kind of ministry (a truly Community-based Enterprise) from the tactic of simply renting out parts of the facility to other groups in order to reduce the net costs of maintaining an old building with a current congregation much smaller than the one that originally built it. The latter is simply a tactic to make a more conventional model of church economically feasible. With the latter, there is rarely a vision of advancing the church's mission itself with regard to the product, services, or memberships that are marketed to the community.[53]

We also wish to distinguish the Community-based Enterprise from an annual church bazaar or rummage sale. The bazaar is not an ongoing enterprise. It is typically an alternative form of giving by church members, where, in addition to cash donations, they give away excess items from their consumerist lives, so as to clean out attics and garages and to make additional money for the church. They may bake cakes or make crafts as well. The latter hints of community-based enterprise, but generally it is a much smaller part of the church's total life and funding. Monies made from such fund-raisers typically are applied to building repairs or to special mission causes. They often work to supplement funds that have been lost as the church has shrunk in its donor base.

Another twist in terms of a retail business in the ministry design is the free store or thrift store, where pulling in direct financial profit is not the main purpose of the enterprise. With mostly volunteer and/or minimum wage workers, a free store is primarily a community development enterprise. Amazing faith communities have developed from free store and thrift store ministries as the workers and customers grew in relationships and began intentionally to converse about ultimate things.

High profile and high impact ministries may function to rally a very wide donor base in the community, far beyond the church members and participants. When a free store ministry helps to inspire hundreds of thousands of dollars in annual community donations (as happens with Church for All People in Columbus, Ohio), it is functioning both to advance the church's ministry and to underwrite it financially. In the latter case, the church is not expecting either the worshipers or the customers to pay all the bills, but is expanding the base of support to community donors who see the good being accomplished in the neighborhood.

As fewer churches are able to grow large enough to support their ministry costs entirely with participant donations, look for a proliferation of Community-based Enterprise churches in the coming decades. This is a key segment of the rising church in North America, especially as the local, recycling, and sustainable practices of the green worldview continue to grow.

THE INNOVATION LAB

WE TRY STUFF. Sometimes things actually work. Some of the people at our mother church probably think we are crazy. They thought we were going to launch a worship service at the cinema. I think some of them are still waiting for that. But the population around here is highly suspicious of organized religion. Few people we talked to were looking for a church, and those who were had already found the nondenominational thing out by the high school. So most of our meet-ups and ongoing groups feel nothing like any experience of church that any of us have ever had.

We tried a family campout in the national park with early morning intergenerational yoga and contemplative prayer. We have a mother-daughter group that has just taken off. All the moms are lesbian. Another group started as a partnership of formerly incarcerated people and their mentors for reentry into life outside prison; but, over time, everybody was mentoring everybody else. Now the group has taken its focus toward raising awareness of needed reforms in the criminal justice system. One of our groups gets together to study the Bible one night each month. The entrance requirement is that you have to have some doubts, so they

do really critical Bible study, no holds barred. Some members of the group are agnostic, but everyone enjoys cutting through the church B.S. to experience the power
and spirituality of the text. That group started as a weekend retreat, and they had
so much fun, they are still going two years later.

One weekend a month, we borrow space from the local Episcopal church,
and we chant and engage in ancient liturgy for an hour. Some of the Episcopalians
join us, and we are never sure who is who. It's not like we keep formal membership
anyway. Yet even with no official membership outside the mother church, some of
these communities that have formed around various mission projects and spiritual
practices have grown very close—friends for life.

Quite a few of the newer faith communities being planted in America
are, in part, Innovation Labs. Much of what they try will be short-
lived or never take deep root. But from their learning, we will
all profit. Every now and then they will discover a promising new approach to engaging people in faith community. There is a maiden voyage
for everything. A lot of them get about as far as the Titanic. Several of the
paradigms of church that we articulate in this book started as experiments.
They were attempted by risk takers who cared about the people who did
not fit or feel drawn to existing expressions of church.

Somewhere out there in the last few decades, somebody invented the
current iteration of what is commonly called "pub theology" (spiritual dis-
cussion over beer or wine). It has accrued about as dependable a track
record of taking root as any new ministry form created in the last thirty
years. If you do it right, it rarely fails. But for every pub theology jackpot
there are a lot of good tries that do not live up to expectations.

Ministry innovation is, more often than not, directed at people who are not currently church participants. Sometimes these folks can be very slow to affiliate with anything remotely organized and religious. Other times, affiliation with the group does not lead to a committed relationship in the same sense as has been typical of church membership in years past. Almost invariably, even when people really gravitate toward the gathering, they do not come with a mindset of financial generosity that would even begin to approach the tithing model.

So it is important that experimental communities are set up to be able to survive a long season before significant funding from participants arrives. The Innovation Lab that sponsors such communities might be a more conventional congregation with very stable funding and the motivation to remain connected to more experimental communities for many years, without the necessity that such communities be quickly weaned. In other cases, where there is no sponsoring congregation, a very lean financial model may suffice where most leaders have day jobs—so that very little payroll and absolutely no mortgage is required in order for the lab to keep trying new things and to keep helping to sustain and stabilize the things that work. In still other cases, private foundations can underwrite robust experimentation.

It is important that denominational offices clearly know the difference between an experimental project and a project with a proven track record in social conditions akin to the mission field in question. A denomination can create an innovation zone to prototype new kinds of faith community in cost-effective ways. When denominations fail to distinguish between the Innovation Lab and the more proven strategies, confusion ensues. When they fund all their new projects equally, regardless of the degree of experimentation and regardless of fruitfulness, they inevitably end up underfunding one thing and overfunding another. On the one hand, a promising and growing faith community, leading its judicatory in new people reached, could suddenly face crippling funding loss after the initial grant is spent. On the other hand, a struggling project that consistently fails to thrive over time could find itself overcapitalized as a long-term venture and continued at full funding for years, when in fact it should have simply been celebrated as a short-term prototyping experiment.

Our own coaching group was born out of a beautiful experience with three Innovation Labs in Washington, D.C., in 2007–09: (1) a Baptist-Methodist midweek worship collaboration downtown, (2) a fellowship of families with deaf children, and (3) an Arlington young adult fellowship that worshiped on Monday nights. All three morphed into other forms within a few years. Fruit was borne. The legacy of this work continues, but in other churches that have been born from or blessed by the work.

Innovation Labs are a critical gift to the world and to the Christian movement in our century. Every new weird ministry begins with a season of experimentation. The planter has an idea, then tries it out, then assesses its effectiveness, and finally adapts it as she tries the next iteration. Eventually she keeps what works and learns from what doesn't. This season of experimentation can last several years as the planter gets to know the particulars of the ministry context. Innovation Labs are not for any group of investors that needs to measure its impact in terms of immediate payback with lots of new church members (conventionally defined). Investing in an Innovation Lab is much like investing in medical research. You may drop a million dollars in medical research and no new treatment emerges, nor is one life saved. But in the end, does it really matter whether developing a vaccine for HIV costs $100 million or $50 billion? The point is getting it done. At any cost, some things are just worth it. The more pertinent question to the existing church might be "Can you put a price on the souls and gifts of the many who are not currently a part of any faith community but who could be?"

THE PILGRIMAGE

I WAS INVITED TO GO to the Scottish island of Iona with a friend after my divorce. She had been before and just raved about the life-transforming experience that she had while there. At first I was hesitant to go because we were to travel with her pastor and a bunch of Christians. I wasn't raised in the church and certainly did not want to be recruited. But on the other hand, I was looking for an experience that would allow me the space to re-create my life after my divorce. I had a hunch that this was to be my path. I laugh now thinking about even using those words—"path," "journey," and "pilgrimage"—because at the time they were so foreign to me.

There is an abbey on Iona dating from the fourth century that was rebuilt about a hundred years ago, where we met for morning and evening prayer. Amazing that this little island spread Christianity to all of Ireland and Scotland. I can't tell you why, but while I was there I felt deeply held in the arms of grace and forgiveness. And I was healed of my grief. They call Iona a "thin place" where the veil between heaven and earth is very thin. I believe it! I actually encountered the love of God as I walked on the holy ground of this island. It was so present, so real. There is a special rock that I sat on every day at the sea and I often go back to this place in my mind when I am going through difficult times. That memory reminds me that I am blessed and helps me re-center myself with a sense of deep abiding peace. I am now comfortable talking about God because I have walked through an experience of holy pilgrimage.

My first experience was so profound that I invited my daughter to come with me on my next pilgrimage. I know deep within that no matter what happens in my life I can trust that God is with me. I look at life so differently now and have learned to discern those waves of grace that flow all around me. Every time I go on pilgrimage I form deep spiritual relationships with other pilgrims. The Celtic phrase for this is *Ana Cara*—soul friend. I am now a part of a larger community of souls who are on the journey of life together, and this humbles me as well as gives me hope.

The first Christian pilgrimages in the fourth century were directed to sites in Palestine connected with the ministry of Jesus. One of the very first was organized by none other than the mother of the Emperor Constantine. Throughout the centuries pilgrimages have expanded beyond the Holy Land to other sites associated with the apostles, saints, and martyrs, as well as the apparitions of the Virgin Mary. But it was not until 1987 when Paulo Coelho wrote his captivating account of his pilgrimage along the road to Santiago de Compostela in Spain that the practice of Christian pilgrimage regained popularity in our era. Now you can find books on pilgrimages along the way of St. Francis of Assisi in Italy as well as to the holy islands of the Celts in Great Britain.

Pilgrimage is not your typical vacation tour experience. Rather it is an intentional process that includes three movements: preparation, experience, and reentry. Preparation can include months of endurance building for walking long distances with a backpack, clearing your calendar, and breaking away from existing commitments and normal routines. The things that normally distract are intentionally set aside so that there is an opening to take on new ways of being. As the pilgrims travel out of their normal routines and enter into the experience of pilgrimage they meet other seekers and form a community of shared experience. This community deepens as they face the adversity of multiple modes of travel that take the pilgrims to new, strange, and wonderful environments. In the process pilgrims encounter all their worst and best selves—doubt, questioning, joy, awe, the dance with control and letting go, the limits of the human body, valley and mountain experiences. They open to trust and awaken to the most unexpected sacraments. They discover the extraordinary in the ordinary. Then the journey back home begins in reverse with time to reflect. Many discover that the life they lived is no longer relevant in light of their pilgrimage experience. Everything becomes new. Their worldview may leap a color forward.

All kinds of journeys could become pilgrimage experiences if we would be thoughtful about them. Mission trips can be a form of pilgrimage if we do homework into the history of the place we are visiting and are intentional about the three movements of preparation, experience, and reentry. The invitation is to open our spiritual senses and look for the tangible feeling of the sacred. The shared experience of mission trips can be a deep community builder with lasting soul friendships.

In 1998, Paul took a group of eleven persons on a pilgrimage to Nazareth in northern Israel, the hometown of Jesus. For a week, the group labored in the sun and dirt on a rocky hillside, working alongside a restoration archaeologist to rebuild agricultural terrace walls of the farms that were in existence when young Jesus was a child running through the olive groves with his friends. The group would rise early, working about six hours until the heat said it was time to stop. Then after a late lunch, they would pile into an old van with a local guide and go wherever their hearts desired—without strict itinerary or tour bus.

At sunset one evening, the group had dinner on the shore of the Sea of Galilee as locals fried fresh-caught fish in little hibachis on the beach below. As the night took hold, lights sparkled from the tops of one of the nearby mountains. Someone asked, "What are those lights up on the mountain?" "That is Zved," said one of the locals. They learned that it was a town more than two thousand years old, and likely sparkled above Jesus and his friends even as he coined the metaphor "A city set upon a hill cannot be hid." Chills ran up arms. On the last day of the pilgrimage, the group stayed the night in an abbey in old Jerusalem. After breakfast, the nuns came with a glimmer in their eyes and keys in hand, saying, "Follow us." They opened a door and the cool smell of cave flowed out. They said that for a couple hundred years, they had been digging under the abbey. The sisters (and a few brothers) had dug down through the layers of time to the actual stones of the original Via Dolorosa of Jesus' day. This was not the stuff of St. Helena's imagination. It was the real road, buried so deep that the tourists never see it. Down in this cave, about twenty feet below the current street level, they had excavated quite a stretch of street. Many of the ancient building facades also had emerged. As the group of pilgrims sat in silence on the benches, one woman suddenly placed her body face first onto the road. Her hands clawed at the stones. No words were needed. All knew. The Lord Jesus had carried his cross on the place where her body was sprawled. After a time, she got up and put herself together. On the way home, she shared that in the numinous encounter on the Via Dolorosa she had received a call from God to create a giant music festival back in the group's home city. When she got home, she rallied friends from many churches, and soon more than ten thousand people gathered in the first year as Grace Fest was born.

This is classic Pilgrimage. It is journey, it is community on journey, it is spiritual reflection and practice in the journey, and it involves a destination that has thin-space character to it. On the journey, something utterly unexpected inevitably happens, and life is never the same for anybody. Commonly there is a call to something significant in the wake of the journey. The experience, and the sense of community, though it may have only a two-week duration, lasts forever. Decades later, when Pilgrimage alums reunite, it may feel as it were only yesterday.

In an era when travel is exploding at a pace far exceeding the growth of population, look for a parallel explosion in Pilgrimage experiences and communities! For many, this will offer the very best experience of church that they will ever find, richly feeding their souls and calling them forth to live as transformed people and conduits of blessing to the world.

SAME TIME NEXT YEAR

THIS IS MY CHURCH. These are my people. And I know that sounds odd because I only see them once a year for this week on the river—but that is how powerful this event is for me. I have made lifelong friends there. And we stay in touch through Facebook and travel during the year. I am always amazed at how much this event transforms me, season after season. The gifts seem to ripple out throughout my entire life. I can see myself differently through the eyes of the people who gather at the river campground; and this has empowered me to make major changes in my life. When we come together, it is almost like we enter into an alternative universe in which anything is possible and I can be who I long to be without any of the barriers that seem to keep me down. I find it hard to share how powerful this experience is for me when I go back home. I guess you just have to be there. But I try to carry the spirit of the experience in my daily life. And as the months pass, I begin to long for my return the same time next year. The time with my people by the river each August is a touchstone in my life.

Same Time Next Year is a classic form of church in America, dating back a couple centuries to the summer camp meetings, where friends would gather for a few weeks of fellowship and powerful devotional practice. The American camp meetings arose in the early nineteenth century when European-heritage settlers were moving across the continent and creating new settlements and towns. During the early days of this westward migration, churches could not organize as fast as the population was swelling. The summer camp meeting functioned as a primary faith community for tens of thousands of these people. It was church. It was vacation. It was powerful community, created for an agrarian society between planting and harvest. Many of the settlers had left family many miles behind on the East Coast or back across the ocean. In young communities, with too few churches organized yet and family often so far away, the camp meeting filled several needs. Over the course of the nineteenth century, as more local churches were planted in heartland communities and affiliation rates rose, the camp meeting shifted in its role. People began to think of it as an add-on experience, a supplement to their experience in, and commitment to, a local congregation.

In more recent times, many of us have experienced Same Time Next Year church through Christian camp and retreat programs. Youth pastors have long observed that the impact for positive personal transformation that comes through a camp experience rivals and often surpasses the impact of week-to-week gatherings, especially for young people in small churches with very few peers.

In the years ahead, such annual gatherings will again become a primary church community for many people. It is happening now with varied experiences ranging from outdoor adventures to yoga retreats, art immersion, rite of passage celebration, and family camps. Within the annual Burning Man gathering in the remote Nevada dessert, there are multiple hubs of community where significant relationships are formed and renewed each summer. Some of these transient villages form around spiritual interests and practices. As fewer people attend weekly worship, such annual events will become a key part of their spiritual growth. Because of social media connections, relationships formed in such events can be preserved and nurtured. We will see events in the years ahead for extended families who want to enjoy the full meaning of Sabbath in terms of playing and praying together, as well as for individuals who are longing for a way to break out of their frenetic lives and begin to ask questions of ultimate meaning for themselves.

One key in marketing these events is to make clear that they are stand-alone rather than a ploy to get people to convert to a certain flavor of Christianity or become members of a local church. The emphasis will be on creating intense experiences of shalom, an alternative way of being in the world that is marked by grace, forgiveness, deep reflection, and possibly emotion. The event will offer a compelling glimpse and a rich taste of the kingdom of God. The memories will become lasting markers for personal renewal and growth.

Even though these events will not typically be directed toward rallying regular worship attendance in established churches, it will be important to intentionally create and gently promote pathways for the ripple effects of such experiences to last well beyond the event. Ripple experiences could be circles that continue to connect via Facebook groups, Google hangouts, podcasts, and webinars. We want to offer the possibility for connection that cultivates our collective memory of the major gathering and invites us to root ourselves in the reality experienced.

Many of the mainline denominations that still have camps as part of their portfolio would be wise to innovate new Same Time Next Year (or next month) experiences that reach out to and connect with the spiritual-but-not-religious. As the churches in these denominations age, there are typically fewer participants in the summer youth programing that was designed for the 1960s and 1970s. The facilities of many camps are also aging, with expensive renovations looming. Many camps will be sold. But we would encourage judicatory groups to be careful in this downsizing. With a little re-visioning, many of these camps and retreat facilities could become major centers of faith and community serving large regions. In some cases, where the alumni rolls of such camps are extensive, churches (of the conventional variety) could be planted that gather a few weekends a year for two overnights at a time. The more people who gather in such spaces for meaningful events, the easier it is to raise the funds to maintain them.

THE COMMUNITY CENTER

"HOW CAN WE PARTNER WITH CHRIST in the unfolding of the kingdom in this community?" That was our overarching question when we began dreaming about ministry in this neighborhood. We spent lots of time meeting the neighbors, non-profit groups, and small business owners in the area. We simply shared our stories and listened. Through that deep listening we began to discover synchronicities of gifts, needs, and passions. We followed those conversations until something began to spring forth. We found nonprofit partners that were helping to bring a sense of shalom to the neighborhood and we began to dream together. Together we transformed a storefront into a place where people can meet to collaborate, whether that be with other nonprofit groups or individuals with a dream. Often we naturally end up working together on projects, fund-raisers, or community advocacy. We have nonprofit partners who help pay the rent, and we are becoming known as the place where good stuff happens for the neighborhood. On Sundays we use the space for worship, and the other days of the week the space is used for arts groups, parenting groups, yoga, community meetings, and 12-step groups. The pastor is also the executive director for the space and chaplain for all the groups.

Community Centers are not new to Christian ministry. But how they are formed in the next thirty-five years will morph. Instead of emerging from a top-down strategic plan, they will more often be birthed out of the context and needs of the community. Instead of ministry to a particular group, it will be ministry with an entire neighborhood, sometimes extremely diverse in its demographic and theological range. These ministries will be resilient as they change with the needs and desires of the neighborhood—no two will look the same.

Pastors in these settings will be community organizers, priests (bridging the sacred and the secular), and, sometimes, executive directors cobbling together their livelihoods from a combination of rental income, grants, programs, and the gathered worshiping community. The ministry lens will be a constant focus on shalom in its fullest sense of peace, wholeness, and health of the neighborhood.

Valley and Mountain Church in Seattle, Washington, partnered with a nonprofit arts group and renovated a storefront in Hillman City with the help of members of a nonprofit homeless youth league who were learning construction skills. They created a co-working space for nonprofits and cultural creatives complete with a conference room, lockers, and office equipment. They transformed a patch of grass in the back of their building into a community garden in cooperation with an urban gardening group. They welcomed the Catholic workers to create a drop-in center and hospitality desk. Currently they have four partners who share the cost of the building in addition to multiple community groups who use their space during the week, offering classes, support groups, and concerts as well as organizing social justice activities and pop-up bakeries for the food bank.

The Mix is a co-working community in partnership with White Rock Church in Dallas. White Rock Church is an aging Anglo congregation in the early days of a renaissance in an eclectic urban neighborhood, with immigrants, artists, and young creatives in every direction. The church kitchen was even renovated as a co-working space for bakers and food entrepreneurs in the area. The Mix executive director, Daryn DeZengotita (affectionately called the Mixologist), is working with White Rock's pastors to develop a co-working space in the church's fellowship hall, with suggested donations for monthly memberships, along with partnerships with dozens of social entrepreneurs. Soon there could be many more people networked in a spiritual neighborhood hubbed out of the Mix than the number who attended White Rock back in its heyday of the 1970s. Buddhist meditation, morning prayer, labyrinth walking, spiritual retreats, and any number of transformational gatherings can occur under White Rock's roof, along with gently expanding participation in the Sunday services. The Mix is conveying all sorts of first-century church values seldom developed in normal churches. These values include shared economy, serving neighbors, and healing the effects of poverty. And yet many church leaders would not recognize the Mix as a church at all.

Yet it is church—a weird one.

Connexion in Somerville, Boston, was birthed out of the sale of an outdated and money-sucking church building. The remnant members of the former church decided to move a few miles down the street toward the urban core. They bought and renovated a storefront and began getting to know the neighbors. They renamed the church Connexion because they wanted to be the connection point in their community. Connexion is building partnerships with government agencies, schools, and nonprofits. They have successfully grown and multiplied Freedom Schools for low-income children in the summers. While their worshiping community is small and growing, their impact on their neighborhood is enormous.

Roots of Faith began out of the prayers of the people at Fox Chapel Church in one of the wealthiest communities in Pittsburgh. The pastor, along with a group of parishioners, began doing prayer walks in Sharpsburg, one of the poorest neighborhoods in their school district. Out of much prayer, conversation, and synchronistic opportunities they rented out a storefront and began a weekly free dinner and a Bible study. Within a year they partnered with a legal aid clinic, the local library, the local enterprise zone, and a community reinvestment group. After two years of community organizing, they are beginning to build a worshiping community with folks living on the margins.

One of the marks of what is sometimes called "the missional church" is that their leaders understand that they have to "cultivate the soil of neighborhood" before they will get very far gathering people into the core ministries of the church. A Community Center operated by the church can help to give form and identity to a sense of neighborhood. As people move into the green value meme, the kinds of spiritual gatherings that will emerge from such neighborhoods will shift markedly, away from conventional forms of worship to a variety of smaller, more sporadic experiences—some contemplative, some serving others, some integrating body, mind, spirit, and relationship.

We also see examples of more corporate starts within the orange worldview.

Gulf Breeze United Methodist Church in northwest Florida was a pioneer in the development of church as a Community Center. In 1999, the church opened a second campus: the Gulf Breeze Community Life Center (now Community Life United Methodist Church). The center opened with a couple thousand people coming through its doors in the first week. Programming was designed in response to community needs and interests. The community was short of "third place" kinds of space (those places of home-like familiarity and community that rank alongside home and work settings as places of significant relational networks). Childcare, recreation, recovery programs, and support groups were primary. Because it was the late twentieth century in the South, about one out of every three people who came through the doors that first week returned to check out the worship service. The church was intentional that they would be a Community Center first, not a Venus flytrap to catch people for Christianity. This is a critical dimension of the twenty-first-century Community Center church. People appreciate the laid-back environment. The Community Life Center worship service was decidedly weird in terms of being so indigenous and out-of-the-box for its time and place. It generated buzz and grew quickly just from word of mouth within the community, growing beyond one thousand weekly worshipers in about six years.[54]

Fast forward fifty years into the middle of this century, however, and a Community Center church will look very different in almost any community, even as the foundational principles may be quite similar.

Cornerstone Centre in suburban Toronto was inspired by the Florida project years earlier. The building is spectacular, their vision clearer than ever, and the culture of excellence equal to that of the church in Florida. It took many years to raise the funds to build the center. In the meantime, they sought "to be the centre they intended to build," across the thirteen years that it took them to secure land, raise money, and build their facility. The focus is on creating community programming—not church programming.

Yet the difference between their center and many others is that the building of community between Christians and neighbors is the point—not converting the neighbors (an overbearing stance) nor simply providing social services (a missional cop-out). They want to build powerful relationships and share stories, trusting God to work in their midst. There is no doubt that Cornerstone Church will grow—they nearly doubled in worship attendance in the first weeks after they moved in. Yet in a city with a bright green worldview, they can expect to draw a smaller fraction of the center participants into the religious life of the congregation. A comparable Community Center church, Redeemer Church in Munich, Germany, has seen steady growth. But fewer participants are entering the church's faith life than likely would have in the last century. As we push further into this century, we expect both of these congregations to thrive. We do not expect that they will become megachurches. (But with Cornerstone, the jury is still out.)

These centers took millions to build and require directors of operations who are managers par excellance—and, in the German example, able to generate tens of thousands of dollars a year in participant fees to help run the center. Where a highly dedicated core congregation can raise the money or where real estate assets from legacy congregations can be leveraged, state-of-the-art facilities are possible. In addition, the pastoral teams in these churches are on top of their game: creative, culturally savvy, and steeped in personal spiritual practice. They design engaging and relevant spiritual experiences for nonreligious people with spiritual curiosity.

For every Community Center church in the twenty-first century that will secure funding to build marvelous public facilities, scores of others will rent or borrow space, and do this on a much smaller scale. The ministry norms for most congregations in the years ahead are going to be significantly smaller in numbers of people than what we were used to in the twentieth century.

The Community Center model of church can adapt to blue, orange, green, yellow, and turquoise worldviews. It is here to stay. We simply caution church leaders to pay attention to its morphing, and to adjust their expectations according to the cultural context.

THE MISSION BASE CAMP

FOR YEARS, our church had been advocating for LGBTQ rights—within the District of Columbia, within the U.S. military, within our denomination. I remember the day we voted to conduct gay weddings, in holy transcendence of the denomination's rules. The day of the vote came after several months of conversation and discernment within the congregation. We knew as we voted that a Yes vote risked our pastor (Dean Snyder) being removed and possibly defrocked. Dean was fearless about the matter. About four hundred members gathered in the sanctuary after worship, with another hundred observers in the balcony. The district superintendent officiated the meeting, according to the denomination's polity. The voting was by secret ballot. They collected the ballots at the front of the room, where tellers would tally the results before the crowd. Yes votes into one box and No votes into another. As the tellers counted, the crowd sang old gospel hymns—likely the same hymns they sang at Dexter Avenue Baptist in Montgomery during the bus boycott in the 1950s. "Blessed Assurance." "Standing on the Promises." We watched ballot after ballot going into the Yes box. At least one hundred ballots went by before one went into the No box. By the end of the fourth hymn, they certified the vote: 397 to 8, and the house erupted in cheers. I realized that day that we were a mission base camp— a community energized by a great gospel cause, where everything we did from worship to Bible study finally called for the question "What are we going to do about it?"

—*A remarkable day at Foundry United Methodist Church, Washington, D.C., in the fall of 2010.*

The Mission Base Camp exists to change the world, according to its vision of God's will for the world. Usually this mission is related to the theme of expanding social justice and the reign of God's grace in the world. In the mid-nineteenth century, the slavery abolition movement animated many churches, rallying the people, defining their vision for a world healed. In the early twentieth century, the women's suffrage movement and organized labor movement played a similar role, galvanizing socially sensitive congregations. In the mid-twentieth century, it was the black civil rights movement. In more recent years it has been farm workers rights, Hispanic civil rights, gay rights, stopping the nuclear arms race, ending human trafficking, and Black Lives Matter. In the decades ahead, the issue of climate change could surpass all previous issues as the single greatest rallying cry in the history of Christianity. The implications of unchecked global warming are enormous for the future of the human race. And the current political structures are as yet largely ineffectual for the fight. So it is likely that people of faith (many faiths) will finally lead the parade in rallying the world toward sanity, and survival. The Roman Catholic Church is definitely stepping up to the plate on this one. There will be certain churches that will rise up with holy determination around particular issues where they sense the time has come to focus and deploy "all hands on deck" toward critical social change.

There used to be a donut/coffee ad in the United States with the tagline "America runs on Dunkin'." Every country, and every community within it, runs on something. The same is true of churches. Some churches run on ecstatic worship experiences (see the Tabernacle), others on tight fellowship (see the Family Chapel), and still others on the advancement of social justice. But the latter churches often move beyond dabbling in multiple causes or in trumpeting social justice as a generic bromide and allow the Spirit to shape them around a particular challenge for a season.

One such church is the Village Church in Toledo, Ohio. The focus of the Village is caring for persons on the margins of power and social acceptance. The Sunday after the Trayvon Martin shooting, they (along with hundreds of other churches) wore hoodies to worship. Another day they all wore purple to show support against bullying of LGBTQ teens. That time, the church held a rally at a busy intersection near their place of worship, and a hundred others from the community came to join them. The passionate embrace of marginalized people brings a diverse cast of beautiful characters into the life of the church. Pastor Cheri Holdridge says, "Every Sunday, it a glimpse of God's kingdom."

The United Church of Christ (of which the Village Church is part) has, throughout its short history, stood at the forefront of witness for social justice and global healing. This small, feisty denomination has proven dependable to offer an early voice for every major social justice cause whose time has come in America. At each turn, where the UCC has spoken loudly, clearly, and prophetically, some of its members and its churches have left the denomination. Many of the causes that it has embraced have seemed quite radical to many people at the time, especially people with blue worldviews. Years later, those same causes can become mainstream social consensus, both within the church community and beyond. When the denomination, or the pastor, takes a stand on an issue in which the local congregation has not yet found consensus, the issue can decimate a congregation. Yet the legacy of this work goes to the middle adapters: the Lutherans, Episcopalians, Presbyterians, and even nondenominational groups. What was edgy in 2010 turns out to be mainstream in 2030.

Sometimes, where a thoughtful conversation has occurred within the congregation, and decent consensus has emerged around a critical life issue, the church may actually gain people because of the stand it takes and/or the passionate commitment that it offers. We saw this in the early days of the gay rights movement. Such a church still may lose a few participants, even as it attracts a new group of participants and reactivates certain participants. The latter people are energized and motivated by the church's position and its advocacy work to advance its point of view in the larger society. The issue (or set of issues) that defines such a church becomes both fuel and rallying point. So that it may then be said, "Grace church runs on the fight for prison reform," and so forth. (Typically, Grace church would also have a ministry team that partners with residents in a particular prison—so that there is a combination of mercy and advocacy in their expression of mission.)

AfterHours Church in Denver pours an enormous amount of energy into blessing homeless people. To date, they have not focused as much on policy advocacy as they have on personally touching and honoring the humanity of their neighbors. At each of AfterHour's five indoor worship locations (in pubs around Denver), a part of the service is to make and pack lunches that will be distributed the next day in the park across from the Colorado State Capitol. The sixth location of the church is outdoors, in the park, where the church gathers 365 days a year at noon, regardless of weather conditions, to share lunch, hugs, prayers, dry socks, and Holy Communion with the downtown homeless population.[55]

Saint Mary's-in-the-Hills Church in Lake Orion, Michigan, settled on the issue of suicide as a major local life need to address on multiple fronts, ranging from loving families who know the pain of suicide to advocating for mental health policies and funding. They are a small congregation, and they chose to make this a signature issue and theme for their church. It is not the whole of their ministry, but a focus of major effort. A church could organize its life around a passion for almost any issue where the grace and love of Jesus Christ has a compelling word.

One important detail: when churches that organize heavily to win single issues in the political arena actually *win the battle*, they may see church participation suddenly fall unless and until they find another issue of social righteousness to embrace or a next mountain to climb with regard to the issue that they have chosen. Bottom line: the Mission Base Camp church cannot thrive without its cause.

Discipleship in such a place means getting involved on the ground, in the world, making a difference. Tending to the management and execution of inner church ministries is important—but the greatest work is beyond the walls. This can create a challenge in terms of recruiting for children's ministry and other necessary teams that almost every church needs in order to function. Everything a Mission Base Camp church does, including children's ministry, will have to be framed in terms of world impact for good.

THE GALLANT FORTRESS OF DEFIANCE

MOST CHURCHES DON'T REALLY TEACH the Bible anymore. Our church is faithful to God's Word. We were raised Lutheran, but those people have totally given in to the culture. They don't challenge you to be anything other than what you would be if you went to no church. What do they really stand for? So it's like, *why waste your time with a church like that?* It means nothing. Its just social stuff and feel good. Our church stands on the Word of God—and it doesn't change with the latest fad. We teach the differences between God's role for men and for women. We don't water down the Bible's teaching about homosexuality. Some of our beliefs may not be popular with the world, and we may not be the largest church around. But this is not a popularity contest. It is, more accurately, a faithfulness contest.

The overall percentage of people with blue worldview in America is decreasing in our lifetimes, probably more than at any other time since the European settlers arrived. And yet the people with blue worldviews remain the most likely to participate in a church. One of the reasons that conservative churches have thrived and often continue to thrive in the United States is that the remnant of our population that continues to attend church is disproportionately blue compared to the total population. In case you have puzzled over why some denominations are actually more conservative today than two generations ago, this is part of what is going on: the portions of their membership that moved into orange and green simply left. When conservative religion or culture takes on a strident and defiant air, we often call it fundamentalism.

Fundamentalists waged an ecclesiastical war to pull the Southern Baptist Convention toward a less culture-accommodating and more culture-defiant posture in the 1980s. They won that battle decisively within that denomination. A generation later, we are now seeing membership decline in the Southern Baptist Convention, rivaling and even surpassing the rate of decline in more liberal denominations. The SBC continued to see slow net membership growth for around thirty years after most of the old denominations began declining—in part because its children were bluer in their outlook than the children of most other American communions. When children grow up to become adults with blue worldviews, they hang on to church more dependably than their friends who may have orange or green worldviews. But now that blue is notably shrinking within the overall culture, churches that pride themselves on doctrinal and cultural hard lines in the sand are coming into tougher times.

They are also vulnerable to the appeal of the Spiritual Theme Park church. The latter is often able to build a "big tent" that can accommodate multiple worldviews. And it's often just a better show. The more liberal denominations have been losing their kids to the nondenominational megachurches for decades. Now the more conservative churches are beginning to get a taste of this.

For true-blue churches to dependably grow in the increasingly secularized society of the next two or three decades, they have to do several things really, really well—with little margin for error. They have to run excellent age-level ministries. One stumble with a bad staff hire in a consumerist age, and they can lose a third of their families. Their constituency wants to raise godly children, and will have no patience with a church that is stumbling in children's and youth ministry. The other challenge is to be able to make a case for their worldview without coming off as too negative (or as "haters"—in the eyes of green value meme people). To the degree that a few high profile pastors have aligned themselves with political movements that are dismissive of certain kinds of people, a few blue worldview churches risk rebranding blue churches everywhere as houses of hate. As this happens, it could speed up the shift from blue toward orange and green in the overall society.

The Gallant Fortress of Defiance, however, doesn't care much about any of that. It is an intense blue-values faith community, less interested in public relations, and more interested in doctrinal and cultural purity. In a world of mealy-mouthed politicians and preachers, the outrageous and flamboyant voices stand out: people who say what they mean, often without much filter. A lot of folks admire leaders who don't seem to care what other people think. Granted, a proud, obstinate stance, focused on hot button issues, may accelerate the marginalization of the larger Christian movement. But at the local church level, in neighborhoods with lots of blue around, a defiant embrace of old-time ideas, values, and language may serve as an effective rallying point.

The people who will gravitate to blue worldview churches in the years ahead are more likely also to choose to withdraw entirely from public education. In some cases, they may withdraw in despair from active participation in the secular political process. They may increasingly interpret their experiences in a secular world in terms of being persecuted for being different and for being true to their tribe's old values (which they usually conflate with God's Word).

The Amish, and to a lesser degree the old Mennonites, offer us the classic models of a pure blue approach to Christianity, without any compromise with orange. There will, inevitably, be new (and softer) variations on the same theme, as new groups seek to create a Gallant Fortress of Defiance against the world's depravity. In the case of the Mennonites, Quakers, and others, their historic commitment to pacifism and peacemaking aligns them with people of green sensitivity.

During the last fifty years, during times of war, there have been numerous faith communities that were gallant fortresses of defiance with a
decidedly green hue, standing up to blue-orange militarism. However, as
green worldview becomes increasingly mainstream, such communities
may lose their historic role as the defiant sect standing up against Goliath.
Or, if the West gets bogged down in a multiyear war with Islamists, we
may see the rise of a new generation of defiant pacifist churches, as robust
as the old Quakers. They could be either blue of green in perspective. Time
will tell.

There will be blue worldview faith communities around for as long as
civilization endures. Look for many of them to become more consciously
and intentionally counterculture, even to the point of cultural defiance. As
countercultural enclaves, they may be less focused on evangelism and
church growth than they might have been fifty years ago in a bluer overall
society. In Islam, as rising global awareness has created tension for blue
Muslim communities, red worldview radicals have emerged ready to assert extreme violence in order to intimidate modernity and to beat it back.
We can only hope that such holy war mentality does not find similar hosts
among blue-worldview Christian groups, pulling them back toward red,
as they process a sense of the culture being under siege from infidels.

And let's remember: the fact that blue worldview is currently declining
in North America is no promise that this trend will continue uninterrupted.
It could all change at any time. A significant trauma (a nuclear terrorist attack on a Western city, a severe economic or food supply catastrophe, or a
sudden, deadly epidemic of a new disease) could create conditions that
quickly increase the attractiveness of blue- (or even red-) worldview religion in the population.

THE SMALL VENUE MULTISITE

AS WE WERE DREAMING about launching Urban Village Church, my friend Christian Coon and I felt God ask us not just to start a new church but also to help develop a new model of church—one that understands creating new communities to be a significant part of the local church's mission. Instead of one large church in one city neighborhood, we envisioned a multisite church of small (one hundred to two hundred people in worship) communities, or sites, meeting in rented or borrowed spaces in diverse neighborhoods throughout our city. These small communities would be powerfully connected as one church with one mission and would share financial and human resources, first-century style; but they would incarnate that mission in contextually indigenous and hyper-local ways. Now five years old, Urban Village is one church with four sites across Chicago, with more than eight hundred active adults involved and around four hundred gathering for worship on any given weekend. Our multisitedness has paid dividends: our clergy and lay leadership are increasingly diverse; there is a fundamentally team-led approach to ministry and therefore a deeper stability in the system; we hold together the power of a large movement with the intimacy of a small community; and we experience a

widening capacity for research and development—our multivalence allows more freedom for risk, failure, learning, and growth.

—*Trey Hall, co-founder, Urban Village Church, Chicago*

Multisite churches have only become common in the last twenty-five years in America. In the early days of the multisite revolution, the standard assumption was that to go multisite, you needed to be a big church. This was because this approach to church expansion was pioneered by high-profile, very large churches. We assumed lots of things in those days—that you needed to own a building, that you needed a different live preacher for each service, or that the pastor had to drive like a mad person through the city to get to each site. We continue to learn much about how a church can spread out effectively over a geographical area. As earnestly as we would like to look with clarity into the future of the church, a la 2050, let's recall what the future looked like back in 1980. Few people (except maybe Lyle Schaller and a few church geeks) even saw multisite coming. It was truly revolutionary—helping to reinvigorate church planting by leveraging the strengths and resources of existing, healthy churches to replicate and innovate ministry. Few of us today can accurately imagine how this will morph in the years ahead.

If, in 1980, or today for that matter, we were to take an offering at our church as a token of support to the new church that the denomination wanted to plant down the road from us five or ten miles, it would be a very small offering—and most of the funds would ultimately come from the denomination or personal friends of the church planter. When our congregation becomes the official sponsor of the plant, the offering gets larger—since we own the mission to some extent. But even then, an "us and them" mentality mitigates our full support. We may even worry that they are going to take some of our most valuable people, or compete with us for new members. These are some of the dynamics that worked to slow down Protestant church planting in the late twentieth century.

However, with the advent of the multisite approach, the energy of the 1970s church growth movement was harnessed to church planting. No longer was the goal of the large church simply to grow larger on one piece of land, but we discovered that a growing church could spread out. By spreading out, we could avoid building a large, very expensive worship arena that would then turn out to be mostly empty within a generation or two. As we have continued to play with the multisite strategy, we have learned that churches do not have to be gigantic in order to reproduce ministry this way. In fact, we now know that almost any size system can reproduce itself in another neighborhood or cultural context. The reproduction can be franchise-like (very efficient and orange in style) and pipe in the sermon and creative work from another site, or it can place a high value on cultivating indigenous expressions of church in each setting (more green).

As we look ahead, we believe that the multisite church is here to stay. In some cases, it will enable strong and culturally adaptive churches to pick up closed church properties and reopen them with a renewed ministry— in some cases preventing a community from losing its last viable house of worship. As is true for the future of the church at large, the future of multisite is varied. We see more video-venue preaching *and* more live preachers in each place. We see more churches choosing hybrids between the two. We see unprecedented integration of online technology with live gathering in all sorts of churches, and this will especially be true of multisite churches—since the latter tend to be proactive about helpful change and innovation. Some churches will think of their online matrix of relationships and gatherings as a virtual campus, with a distinctive campus pastor. For others, the web interactions will permeate everything, so that such a clear delineation would be impossible.

The vast majority of new multisite gatherings will be small venue, with less than two hundred people in each place, often as few as fifty. Most of these gathering hubs will be created without the purchase of property. The typical twenty-first-century multisite church will either own no property or own one home-base ministry center. Those that own or lease multiple properties may simply receive donations of closed church buildings or find low-cost pieces of commercial real estate. In the latter case, the fifteen-hundred-square-foot storefront space may simply serve as a basecamp for daily ministry presence in the neighborhood, and not as the worship venue (since it is too small).

This is the age of borrowed space, rented space, shared space, and the like.

You may observe that one church could embody several of the paradigms outlined in this book. By midcentury, for example, it may be hard to imagine a vital church that is not working and thinking multisite to some degree. This reflects a revolutionary shift beyond the twentieth-century idea that a church was a group of people who met in a particular building with their name on it.

21

THE TABERNACLE

WE STAND IN LINE for a about a half hour each Sunday afternoon to get in. We have learned to expect something wonderful each week. You can feel God in the worship (that is, the music) and in the altar prayer time. Sometimes, in the midst of the praise, you will hear someone in the room blow a ram's horn. The first time I heard it, it was like a rhino roaring. Miracles happen in that place. The people are from all over Latin America—some of them work two jobs to make ends meet. But who would not have time for something like this each week? God is in the house.

The Tabernacle is the place where people gather for worship and leave with a sense that they have touched God. It is thin space. As we learned in our glimpse into Pilgrimage, thin space is a time and place where the distance between heaven and earth almost dissolves. Tabernacle is a classic American religious tradition, dating back to the summer camp meetings and the seasons of Great Awakening. The black church in America also emerged with a strong sense of Tabernacle, a tradition that continues in many congregations. *There is something decidedly anti-institutional about the Tabernacle*, which is why it is of special interest to us as we imagine the future of religion.

People in the green worldview can sense emotional manipulation and contrived hype a mile away. But when there is no manipulation going on, when the worship experience is simply a good faith effort to open ourselves corporately to experience the presence of God, the most eclectic assortment of human beings can wind up in the room, from the young brainy community organizer trying to increase high school graduation rates to the ER doctor to the undocumented construction worker.

Yes, some churches will seek to manufacture a sense of God's presence mechanically, with a certain type of music, mood lighting, and even dry ice (seriously). Much of the time, in our observation, it falls flat, and just feels like trying too hard. We don't see a lot of future in that. Some of what we today call contemporary worship is really just painful to watch, and especially so for younger people. You can't create thin space "painting by the numbers," especially when it is baby boomers painting for millennials.

But there are times and places where the pieces fall together, never entirely of human doing. A serendipity of worship emerges that transcends all the best planning: a certain inspiration and energy that feels magical. And people begin to expect an encore experience week after week.

Communities that experience this kind of worship-oriented thin space are special places. In these Tabernacles, worship moves beyond the script into a true sense of encounter with the Holy. Such places are magnetic—always. Purple, red, blue, orange, green, or yellow, it does not matter the worldview. Except, we would say, that we have few examples yet of where this exists without a good base of blue in the room. We don't know that many turquoise-worldview people yet—but they are mystics—and people living in turquoise may be attracted to Tabernacle like moths to a flame. Or not. We shall see.

When people experience true Tabernacle, it is always compelling. A lot of folks are distrustful of it and closed to it, for any number of reasons. Such folks will never go near it. But we will probably continue to be surprised by the faces that suddenly show up in Tabernacle places in the future, including some of our children. The more secularized a society, and the less religious exposure a person has, the more apt many folks will be to try new experiences (from yoga to raves to mind-altering drugs to ecstatic spiritual experience) and judge such experiences on their immediate merits.

Much focus is placed upon the role of music in such settings, but we must also recognize that when the Spirit is pulsing in a room with an electric quality, it is also a wonderful place to preach or to share one's faith story. Words take on an extra dimension of credibility and authority. Very ordinary sermons take on a certain sweetness and power. And there is nothing that the preacher has done to create this, other than just the basic preparation she would do anyway. It is like a surfer just waiting for when the good waves come. When they come, you just want to be ready.

The Tabernacle is a worship-centered paradigm of church, all about experiencing God tangibly. In the goose bump zone, the Christian faith often becomes very interesting again to those who may have grown listless or disgusted by organized religion earlier in their lives. Thus we should not be surprised to see the enormous magnetism of the Hillsong churches in Sydney, London, and New York City or megachurches in all sorts of places, where worship attains a special energy and sparkle.

For the moment, much of the music being written for such places comes from the blue worldview, heavily steeped in the salvation-from-shame genre, focused on Jesus' dying as a sacrifice to enable God to save us, and still decidedly masculine in its God imagery, This kind of theology is deeply off-putting to people with green values. We suspect that a new generation of incredibly evocative and inspirational music (in the black music tradition and also the American evangelical contemporary tradition) will emerge with more theological nuance—enabling all parties to relax and open themselves more fully to the Presence. This critical shift will enable the Tabernacle to continue as a major (and possibly growing) segment of American religious life by midcentury.

Look to the innovators to integrate the sounds and beat from every sort of contemporary dance music. Look for some to weave in contemplative practice—these places do not have to be all noise! They are typically houses of prayer above all else. The possibilities of how the Tabernacle might morph are almost endless.

In Savannah, Georgia, an old church called Asbury Memorial lives on the fringe of its denomination. It has embraced hundreds of people across the years who would not be in any church on Sunday, save for the fact that Asbury has created a Tabernacle where grace and hope come to life. The church's radical inclusivity and its willingness to bust free of the stifling sense of propriety experienced in many southern American churches make it a place of fresh air. A church that used to gather barely thirty folks now often gathers ten times that, even packing the house on special days. It is anything but a Hillsong kind of place. On a recent Sunday, forty choir members danced down the aisle dressed as fairy tale characters, singing Smashmouth's "I'm a Believer!" The church creates endless iconic moments in people's lives, with the gospel artfully intertwined with every prayer and song. One of the members, Ginger, said, "I'm not a religious person. If it were not for this place, I would not be in a church. I can find God in my garden. But I'm here, instead."

Tabernacles are compelling.

For people whose day-to-day lives are difficult, who may be burned out on (or bored with) hedonistic pursuits, for people seeking recovery from chemical dependency, for people who are exasperated with just playing church, for folks going through major life transitions, or for those who just accidentally walked through the door—the Tabernacle may offer the Surprise of their lives, both antidote and alternative for them: a God high.

THE CATHEDRAL

THIS MAGNIFICENT BUILDING was the Anglican cathedral in Shanghai. It was closed by the communist government and turned into a movie theater for propaganda films. Later it was chopped up into offices for the Communist Party. Then the law changed a few years ago, declaring that any property that had been seized from a church had to be given back to religious use. But it could not be given back to any church whose main office was outside of China. So we (the Three Selves Patriotic Movement Church) petitioned to receive the building, since the Anglicans could not. The building will open in six weeks. We have raised funds from around the world for the restoration. The Koreans donated over a million dollars for the pipe organ. It will be standing room only in here the day that we open. And within a few weeks, we will be full in multiple services. There is such a hunger for faith in China—and in particular, for majestic liturgy and pageant surrounding faith.

—A representative of the national Chinese church, giving Paul Nixon and Justin Kan
a private tour of the Shanghai Cathedral in Lent of 2011, just before it reopened.

Cathedrals are special places: Soaring space, art glass, sometimes dating back almost a millennium, and haunting dances of light and shadow.

In an era when life expectancy was less than forty years, education was reserved for priests and nobility, and a bad flu year could take out one fourth of the town's people, a cathedral served to offer hope. Sometime around the year 1000, advances in engineering made possible the creation of soaring houses of worship, all across Europe. These magnificent structures were built slowly, usually over many decades. Thousands of craftspersons between the years 1000 and 1800 spent their entire careers, from adolescence until death, working on the same building, dying decades before its completion.

Today on a typical Sunday, many of these houses of worship have more tourists roaming around the edges than they have worshipers.

People may assume that the age of the cathedral is done.[56] We heartily disagree. In fact, given how well some of these places are built, many are not even halfway through their practical life, with possibly countless centuries yet before them, and with the endowment to insure ministry virtually into perpetuity.

Even among people with a green worldview, who almost universally resist organized religion, cathedrals have a special lure and offer a sense of holy mystery. European backpackers on a warm summer afternoon are quite apt to seek respite in a magnificent cathedral space. Even in Scandinavia, historic worship facilities are often much more versatile than the typical American church sanctuary: functioning as a venue for majestic worship, contemplative worship, community gatherings, seminars, and concerts (both secular and spiritual).

Last year, we (Beth and Paul) worked together as consultants with a Los Angeles church that was blessed with a magnificent, expansive worship space. Over the years, the generation who built the space moved away or died. Attendance dipped to a fraction of what it was half a century earlier, perhaps below what we might typically consider critical mass for a worship gathering in such a room. But the church took careful note of the changing times, shifting toward a more expansive theology, endowing the choral ministry, upgrading the pipe organ, and investing in someone who could play the instrument. The pastor developed a preaching style that connects biblical themes to everyday life and contemporary culture. The worship planner integrates smart references from the arts. Banks of candles are available along the sides of the worship space, inviting anyone to light a candle and pray for loved ones and world affairs. After the service, quality refreshments are offered, with people spilling into the church courtyard in gentle conversation, followed by a faith conversation group, often moderated by a local theologian. Recent facility renovations include a free parking garage and ultra-contemporary restrooms reminiscent of the nearby Getty Museum. Obviously, it has taken some serious money to do all of this, but the pews in this church are getting a little more full year after year. And, for multiple large donors, the growing crowd makes this cathedral-style ministry seem a worthwhile investment.

Not every church with a soaring and majestic worship space will be able to find the funds or the participants to justify ongoing renovations necessary to maintain it. One church in Maine sold their historic building to a developer who developed a restaurant in the nave, with food openly prepared in the area that used to house the choir. That church chose a different ministry model, embracing a much smaller building footprint in which to base its ministry, and then growing notably from there.

But from Cologne Cathedral in Germany to Yorkminster in the UK to Riverside Church in New York City to the National Cathedral in Washington to Christ Cathedral in Orange County, California, these amazing places will continue to draw together both pilgrims and congregations for centuries to come. The Cathedral church is here to stay, along with a few other more primitive varieties of church, such as the Simple Cell, probably until the end of time.

The Cathedral and the Family Chapel are perhaps the most building-enmeshed kinds of churches. But Cathedrals have an opportunity to make the move from settlers to people on spiritual journey as surely as any other kind of church. By midcentury, anytime you find a full cathedral space, you will almost invariably find a theology as expansive as the room itself. We have observed that every church needs something solid to hold onto, offering a steady footing from which to innovate and change. Evangelical churches with somewhat archaic theology are often the most innovative when it comes to social media and contemporary arts in worship. More liberal congregations often hold on to hymn books and fight video screens like medieval knights rallying to protect the king. Cathedral space can serve a faith community as the ancient grounding that makes possible creativity and exploration of new practices, new ideas, and new syntheses of ancient traditions. Our prediction: As more of the population moves into yellow and turquoise worldviews, the Cathedrals better get ready for an Easter crowd.

THE SPIRITUAL THEME PARK

WE STARTED COMING HERE because our daughter's friends were all coming here. Have you seen the children's area? There's a whole video wall as you pass the check-in station, and a real-time interactive center with children's ministries all over the world. And then the kids go down a giant slide into children's church, where they meet holograms of Bible people, walking all over the place. I don't know where they find all these creative people that do all this. After our first week, our daughter came into our bedroom at seven AM the very next Sunday and asked when we were going to leave for church. We had not even planned to go back that soon. But she was hooked.

And of course, the service for the adults is amazing too. The music. Oh my God! It's like concert quality. And our pastors are all such great speakers—plus they use video in the sermon that takes us to the Bible places where all of the stuff happened, on a big screen. They weave it all together. I never imagined church could be so crazy interesting. It always applies to your life. We have invited a bunch of our friends here. They usually reply that they think church is boring. We tell them, "You just have to see this once, and tell us it's boring." They all love it.

We are building a new state-of-the-art worship arena right now. The people of the church raised over ten million dollars last year to build it, with that amount matched by a Christian billionaire. They say the technology will be over the top. We can't wait.

In the last year, we have gotten more involved. Its amazing how much more there is here than just the Sunday morning. They have organized classes and groups for everything you can imagine. We are even co-leading one now for families with adopted kids. They taught us everything we needed in order to be able to lead the group. They even gave us an ID card, like on a cruise ship—you can swipe it to make a donation, to sign up for stuff. It's a spiritual Disneyworld.

Welcome to the Spiritual Theme Park. It is the megachurch, with mid-twenty-first-century technology. People from traditional churches continually scratch their heads wondering why, in a secularizing age, so many people gravitate to such places—even in parts of the country where church attendance is plummeting overall.

The reasons vary. The number one reason Americans choose church participation (of any kind) is for their children; and megachurches do children's ministry at a spectacular level of performance, thus drawing large enough numbers of children to make the whole place a party. Even though the doctrinal details of most megachurches would be a turn-off to many young adults, such details are often soft-pedaled. The service content is extremely life-practical in terms of teaching and romantic in terms of music. The worship services offer a spiritually therapeutic experience that even people with light interest in religion often find engaging.

The Spiritual Theme Park is designed for a consumerist entertainment-oriented culture, in which the standards of quality entertainment are rising rapidly. In terms of the Spiral Dynamics colors, this church exists in the land of orange! A close examination of the largest churches in America reveals that they are much more likely to reach young adults than smaller congregations. Many of these young adults have some church-participation history in blue-worldview churches. They represent a good percentage of the remnant church participants among the millennials.

But, lets remember: almost *everyone* makes a pilgrimage to Disney with their kids at some point if they have the financial means to do so. This is the nature of mass entertainment culture. The same may increasingly be true of the Spiritual Theme Park church. Count on the core theology to remain a bit like a stiff Scotch for people of green worldview, so that they may not fully swallow in one gulp. But also count on them to give their children a taste of every multisensory experience that they can afford—and in this case it doesn't hurt that there are positive life lessons thrown in for no extra charge.

The market for all churches will become much more challenging in the next few decades. This is true even for the megachurch—which is why we believe that many will morph toward increasing consumer-consciousness in ministry design, and toward cutting-edge technology. This may repel a lot more people than it attracts. But it will continue to drum up a crowd. The jury is still out as to whether the megachurches will become increasingly cultural islands in a secular society or if (in the true spirit of orange worldview) they will continue to morph in terms of changing cultural norms and values. The answer may well be yes to both questions.

Australia is of particular interest to us, in that they are a much more secularized society, with many more people living in a green worldview—possibly offering us a glimpse of America by midcentury. And we see the very large church as one of the last survivors in Australian church life, even as the small mom-and-pop churches close one by one. Maybe the first half of the twenty-first century is simply the era of the big box retailer.

The Spiritual Theme Park church is designed for such an era. Even if its total market share never exceeds 10 percent of the population, that would still be more than a million people in the Los Angeles region, for example. And it would not surprise us to see up to a third of that (or three hundred thousand people) involved in a single state-of-the-art multisite congregation in LA by midcentury, with branches in cities around the world, even as overall church participation continues to drop.

The other thing to remember when it comes to this very market-savvy form of Christianity is this: Every morning, people's hearts are broken and their hopes are crushed. The Christian faith offers a compelling vision of hope for people in these tender moments of life. The Spiritual Theme Park church, with its high visibility and well-executed gatherings, is likely to be one of the places where some people will turn in the tough times, even if just for a season of their lives.

For all of these reasons, we see the large market-driven church as here to stay for decades yet to come. Even though this would seem an anomaly, given the cultural shifts we have explored, please remember that a very savvy megachurch can incorporate multiple aspects of weird church into its program. These people read the marketplace. One thing we can count on with near certainty is that megachurches will morph in this century, in many cases doing whatever is required to hold the attention of a diverse and distracted public. In order to stay in the consumerist religion game, big money will be required.

THE SEMINARY

BEFORE I STARTED at my current church, I had been in and out of churches for thirty years and I still could not tell you much about the Bible. And I never knew how much happened in history between Bible times and now. Nor could I tell you the ways that Christianity differed from Buddhism, or how it has similarities. That has all changed. Not only has my faith grown in the last few years. But I have a framework now. I understand how things fit together. Being a part of a true learning community has opened my eyes to so many things about the core of what Christianity is, as well as to the insight it offers to the world for almost every challenge we face. It also has inspired me to make some major life commitments in terms of how I want to channel my energy, my prayers, and my resources to make a difference.

The seminary has been around a long time. It has roots in the Jewish synagogue, where much energy was spent upon learning the Torah and understanding its appropriate applications for human life. There was (and often still is) an intellectual edge to a synagogue that many Christian faith communities can hardly imagine.

Many of us have memories of seminary kinds of experiences, whether we attended a theological school or were simply a part of a week-to-week church with a very high value for critical thinking. In such places, the most familiar scriptures and theological ideas often leap to life with resounding relevance and hope—so that everything looks different as we walk out the door to go home. Good seminaries are, by nature, exhilarating places. Once one has been exposed to the power of the theological "ah-ha" to reorder and renew life, it is very likely that person will keep coming back for more.

We often don't even think of seminary as a type of faith community, but rather as just a training place. Time to rethink that! The denominational leaders often bemoan the seminaries as the *problem*—the place where faith is taken away or a place so detached and ivory tower that its graduates are clueless to do anything helpful in the world. *This is true irony*: that the people most highly invested in the present forms of church would level such a charge. The denominations often see their steadily declining franchises as somehow more relevant to life than disciplined faith communities committed to learning and deeply rethinking faith. Many theological seminaries refuse to function simply as technical colleges rolling out another batch of pastor-CEOs for the dying franchises. Their bigger mission is to awaken fresh, intelligent, and heartfelt faith in their students, connected with centuries of tradition that have come before us. They trust that from that awakening, God will do amazing things in students' lives—often more amazing than simply maintaining and gently reviving docile and declining institutions.

Even as the number of young adults interested in parish ministry is dropping, some seminaries are thriving and growing younger by the year. One of us teaches occasionally at a theological school and has noted a rising number of students investing in theological education without committing to the conventional professional track of leading denominationally based congregations.

In the bleakness of the 1930s, even as the Nazis were consolidating power and most of the German churches were passive and/or complicit, a young man named Deitrich Bonhoeffer envisioned a different kind of church: a "Confessing Church," he called it. The Confessing Church began just the way Jesus' original movement began: with a group of young leaders entering into covenant together to learn together and share life for a few years—in this case via an alternative seminary that Bonhoeffer established near the Baltic coast of northeast Germany. The point of this seminary was that it would move beyond the simple head trip that most European seminaries encouraged. It would move beyond simply the exchange of great ideas, to *a mixing of great ideas and practice*. That seminary lasted just a few seasons before the Nazis closed it. But it was a birthplace for the twentieth-century Protestant discipleship movement that continues to gather steam worldwide. Some fundamentalist groups took hold of Bonhoeffer's model of integrating learning and practice and sought to adapt it to settings where freedom of thinking and questioning was quite limited (not at all Bonhoeffer's vision of a discipleship community). Others sought to co-opt discipleship as a training for lay leadership within established, perfunctory, institutional churches. Despite all of this, a gigantic paradigm shift from membership to discipleship continues to advance around the world. We are fans!

Be on the watch for new learning-discipleship communities that form beyond the worlds of fundamentalism and formal academia. Watch for heavy-duty theologians who increasingly invest in theological education projects and communities beyond the traditional degree-granting institutions. Elaine Heath is one such theologian who understands the importance of this kind of practical training and spiritual formation. She and Larry Duggins, with the help of many others, have created the Missional Wisdom Foundation, which offers an affordable two-year academy in missional wisdom for people all over the country. Watch for more innovations such as Hatchery LA, a blend of seminary and MBA. Hatchery fashions itself as "an incubator for common cause communities." Assume that much of the teaching and attendant dialogue in such communities will happen via the web. Watch for communities that set their focus upon integrating learning and faithful living, with little interest in the maintenance of conventional church programmatic ministries. When persons of a green, yellow, or turquoise worldview engage the Scriptures and classical Christian traditions, there often emerges a far more socially subversive version of Christian faith, deeply rooted in the ancient traditions. This is one of the most promising forms of weird church that will unfold in the days before us.

Some Seminaries will focus on short-term community, where participants come for a set season to share their lives and to experience spiritual and theological formation, from which they will move on to careers of serving others, with or without pay. Watch for Seminaries that train leaders in both spiritual leadership and in trades and skills to equip competent bivocational pastors in an era of falling church donations. Look for more night classes, more retreat weekends and summer intensive weeks, as people manage to balance these pursuits with other life responsibilities and interests. Some Seminaries will be ongoing congregations, where learning and ministry practice/prototyping are the most important thing they do, even ahead of worship services. Some Seminary communities may gather for large venue worship only a few times a year. Others will gather daily.

Many churches already are shifting toward a life coaching/equipping emphasis. They may claim taglines such as "we help people follow Jesus" or "we get you ready to change the world." In every case, there is a deep learning community at the heart of these churches, along with opportunity for people to test drive what they are learning in real life. When they worship, it is the community's authentic response to a deepening relationship with God, celebrating the growing sense of God's call upon the individuals and upon the community as a whole.

Seminaries generally do not specialize in large gatherings of people sticking their toe in the waters of faith. We may see exceptions to that in the years ahead, where a few churches do "Seminary lite," with theological newbies, marketing to a wide audience. But we expect the norm for the Seminary community to remain *small* and *intense*. And we can expect that after two or three years in such a community, the people in whom they are investing will be unable to stop themselves from diving into all sorts of ministry endeavors across the planet, powerfully formed and ready, with or without a degree.

Think Jesus and the twelve, and you have it.

THE MOMENT OF GRACE

OUR DENOMINATION PICKED US to plant a new church. We went to the church planter training. We had our plan all down, but from the moment we hit the streets in our community, nothing went according to expectations. By the end of the first year, we had only about a third of the people we had hoped to collect, so we postponed launching a public worship service, creating grave anxiety in the denominational office. However, our group gathered weekly in various homes, and we began to have the most amazing conversations. We developed a great relationship with the nearby elementary school. We started a teacher's pantry in the school, where teachers could write on the whiteboard any supply that they needed and our little church would provide it. By the second year, we had about thirty people, not enough to support a pastor's salary or to buy a building, but each gathering felt like the best experience of church any of us could ever imagine. By year three, the denominational officials were pacing fretfully, trying to discover how to close us down, to "pull the plug" as one of them put it. Lucky for them, several of our members got jobs in other cities and a couple went off to graduate school. Three moved away for marriage. So that it seemed to us that we were winding down.

One night we had our final dinner together and the gathering lasted six hours. We are still connected on Facebook—and it would seem that almost all of us are involved in leadership of other ministries and great community projects all across the country. The denominational officer wanted to come and write up a report that he called an autopsy. We refused to cooperate. We all agreed to clam up and tell him nothing. Because we do not consider our twenty-seven-month Moment of Grace a failure—and we don't perceive that anything died. Four different people came to faith in Christ. We all grew to new depths of understanding and community connectedness. The seeds planted continue to bear amazing fruit. And we refuse to cooperate with any analysis that is based in spurious assumptions that blind people to the obvious: that this was all of God.

The Moment of Grace is a faith community that is short-lived. Not every community lasts for generations. Indeed, Jesus' original community of twelve had a three-year run, this assuming Jesus found all the Apostles immediately after his baptism, which is questionable. The original post-Pentecost Jerusalem church was an offshoot of the Apostle's fellowship, but a distinctly new community. One thing led to another thing. So it has always been in Christianity.

Furthermore, every individual faith community has a finite lifespan. That Jerusalem church back at the headwaters of the Christian movement eventually vanished, aided in great part by Roman persecution. Every church that St. Paul planted in what is today Turkey vanished centuries ago. And yet those faith communities are our spiritual ancestors. We are direct descendants.

Every faith community that forms, with its identity shaped around the Christ event, is of God. As with human beings, some may live a few months and others more than a hundred years, but they are equally precious in God's sight. From God's perspective, the whole previous two millennia are but a moment of grace. And church fruitfulness in terms of legacy and global impact may be unrelated to the length of a community's formal existence (exhibit A: Jesus and the original twelve).

Many of us have belonged to such churches. We may not have thought about them as churches at the time, but, in hindsight, we may now be able to see more clearly. Just because there was never a building and an annual budget does not mean it was not profoundly the church of Jesus Christ expressed in a particular time and place and people.

It may have been at summer camp, where over a period of four or five days, amazing trust and transformational community formed, with an impact that still gently forms us and perhaps even offers to us a sense of spiritual GPS decades later.

It may have been in college, where during our freshman and sophomore years we became engaged in a student fellowship connected to a group of donor churches, but which was also church in its own right. We knew from the day it all began at the start of a school year that we would be scattered across a continent and beyond within nine months. So what?

Or it could have been that week our mission team spent in Appalachia working to bring flush toilets to Mrs. Brown's little house. Each day as she made lunch for the workers and we ate on her front porch, it was like Holy Communion. By week's end, we were all family, bound by heavenly connections. And we had become witnesses to a common experience that was as powerful a sign of the coming reign of God as anything we would ever again experience in this life. Friends, that is church.

In the waning days of Christendom certain kinds of faith communities got labeled "para-church." This is a most interesting term. "Para" means "beside." To call something para-church means that we see it as something that comes alongside a church, that exists in partnership or at least, we would hope, in a constructive complementary relationship to a church. In a post-Christendom, postinstitutional era, the term makes almost no sense anymore. In fact the term owed its brief popularity to American denominational churches, fast losing their grip and control on the breadth of Christian faith community. To label something as para-church meant that it was less than a real church, due possibly to (1) lack of formal membership, (2) lack of the classical Christian sacraments, (3) the short-term, transient nature of its life, and/or (4) the number of members of denominational churches who participated in its activities.

It was assumed in those days that you could only properly belong to one church at a time—which so far as we can tell was simply a denominational power ploy to keep control of people and to retain a claim on as much of their tithe as possible. There is no biblical teaching that goes anywhere near this modern concept.

There are powerful Moments of Grace that blossom both within and beyond the structures of institutional churches. We do not see this changing in the twenty-first century, except that we believe our children may take these churches more seriously than did our grandparents. Our children will not likely see these as sideshows, as adjunct communities, nor as rogue groups lacking the full legitimacy of a church because they will not bow to some ecclesial authority. In the postmodern context no ecclesial authority retains the public credibility to make unilateral judgments about legitimacy and get away with it.

Some short-lived faith communities develop their life and work in partnership with established churches. Others spin into existence from a convergence of seemingly random connections catalyzed by the Holy Spirit. There is no better example of the latter than the Day of Pentecost itself; nobody authorized it, funded it, or planned it. It was crudely organized, in that Jesus' disciples found some way to baptize three thousand people. But within a week, it is relatively safe to say that most of those baptized were many miles away, headed in disparate directions, never again to be meaningfully reassembled.

But how silly it would be, especially in this moment of history, to assert that Pentecost was a failure, or that Pentecost was unsustainable, or that Pentecost was not fully church. Pentecost was more than just Christian Woodstock. It was every bit the consummate Moment of Grace.

And when little Pentecosts happen, *as often they do*, post-Christendom followers of Jesus will increasingly view them as a form of church.

THE HOLOCRACY

OUR CHURCH NEEDED TO DO SOMETHING in order to reestablish its connection with the neighboring community. We decided to do a "pilot" project because nobody was sure of any direction or strategy. My only prayer was to discern whether this effort was in alignment with God's plan. Without any assurance of success or expectation, we simply stepped into an unknown territory, full of anxiety and anticipation at the same time.

As soon as we made that first step into the unknown space, I experienced something that I had never experienced before. It is something like this: a boy who cannot dance, although he badly wants to be a good dancer, enters his house and into a grand hall and finds his parents, sisters, and brothers dancing altogether so gracefully, inviting him to dance with them. The boy does not fear to dance any more but naturally joins them in a magical harmony and dances freely with them as if he has always been a great dancer.

This project has helped me see what God has been working on and recognize God's invitation to me into what God is up to. It feels like dancing with the Triune God who is already dancing in a circle to a beautiful music. My project has become a search for the dancing God and led me to join God's dance—"perichoresis." My

prayer changed from discerning God's will or asking God to work on my plan to keeping up with the dance with God.

—*Paul Moon, pastor, Broken Builders Church, New York City*

There is a very different church arising in this young century. We see only glimpses, but it is more than our imagination. Like the European ships that only the eighteenth-century shaman could see on the east coast of Australia—that most of the Aboriginal people could not see—some of us see the Holocracy arising.

And not just in the church. It is the future of organizational development. It is mainstream stuff for our children and grandchildren. But not for us. To most of us it is still weird, very weird.

Imagine a church with thirty pastors, all of whom have the same title and a comparable salary, but with different roles that cover the gamut, based more on their gifting and call than an organizational hierarchy of corporate tasks. Some are ordained, some not. Some have been to seminary, some not. Some take a full time salary, most not. And imagine that one of them holds the rest of them accountable and receives the reports from their work, not because she is the CEO of this operation, but because she is a part-time pastor within the team who happens to have the gift of coaching and oversight. Two of the thirty are Jewish rabbis, and one is a Zen Buddhist. All are on staff in leadership in a decidedly Christian church.

Imagine a lead pastor who understands his major responsibility as holding in place the conditions and practices that make creative expression possible, even as he casts a community vision around simple, elegant, and Spartan rules of common life. And imagine that he also turns in his work plan to the aforementioned part-time pastor, hired only eighteen months ago.

Imagine a church where some of the worship services and gatherings are explicitly Christian in identity and orientation, while others are conversational between Christianity and many other schools of thinking and faith. And the only thing that determines if the church will sponsor it or do it is a simple question—*will a self-identifying follower of Jesus be in the room as part of the conversation?* And that's it.

Imagine a church where the lead pastor's role is rarely, if ever, to drive change from the top. But rather, the challenge is to *hold in place the conditions* in which the newest voices emerging in the community can be heard. And *to see to it* that the persons on the cutting edge of interface between the church and the culture are given the space they need to innovate. This is a church where persons on the edge of the community's organizational life are welcomed and really empowered to invent the church's next iterations and to articulate its next great ideas. The lead pastor listens, listens, listens, and when she hears music, she serves as the amplifier so that a diverse church in thirty locations can all hear it and learn to sing it.

Paul Moon again: "As technology occupies the center of the transformative process of the modern world, it is no longer the case that culture, skills, information, knowledge, and even wisdom flow in one direction, whether it is from older generation to younger generation or from creators to users. Instead, they may be created and transferred by anyone." With this discovery, leadership at Broken Builders Church in New York City began to invite and celebrate innovation from the margins of their community. As a result, in a fourteen-month period, community development went viral across New York City, with nine new multicultural, multigenerational worship communities created in four locations. Leaders and spiritual entrepreneurs with no previous connection to Broken Builders have been appearing out of nowhere to help, with twenty-two pastors now on board, as a movement explodes across the city. And none of it was planned.

Imagine a church where they have never voted on anything from the day it began. Not one vote. The pastors pray, listen to one another, set aside ego, and discover consensus (rarely unanimity, but always consensus). All have an equal voice, regardless of tenure, education, or age. And imagine that this same group of pastors chose a few years back to work with an ongoing advisory group of young adults, a careful mix of Christians and others of good will, so that reverse mentoring can take place, and so that the organization will not grow too old too fast in its generational perspective.

For those familiar with the contours of university life in recent decades, this may at first seem similar—as church-owned and chartered schools of higher education secularized. There is similarity, and then great dissimilarity, for the purposes of church and university ultimately diverge. The purpose of a university is help students to study, to learn to think, and to prepare for gainful employment and leadership. The purpose of a church is more specifically about birthing new life and a new world within the vision and spirit of the gospel. A church is about helping to announce and to invite the kingdom of God into life.

Imagine a church—not a university—where all the people in each cell and circle are rallied toward daily practices of prayer and/or meditation, and daily practices of kindness, forgiveness, and peacemaking. Where it is all about spiritual practice, regardless of the programs, the theological convictions, or the lack thereof. In this church, the community never becomes secular, ultimately because there is no blue and orange food fight over doctrine. It is not an all or nothing between competing truth claims. Here, in this community, the truth of Jesus stands on its own feet, without need for defense or polemical argument.

Such communities will arise as more people move into yellow and turquoise value systems. These folks currently represent a tiny fraction of the population, but that will very likely change in the years ahead.

In the yellow value meme, people move beyond the need to engage in arguments about right and wrong . They become much more able and willing to consider the context and to view the world through the eyes and experience of others. Even as the green worldview gets terribly frustrated by blue and orange expressions of faith community, yellow takes us to a higher tier, where we can appreciate the value of life in each worldview. We may begin to appreciate words of certain old hymns expressed from a blue perspective, perhaps viewing them metaphorically. We also can appreciate and share in the commitments to social justice, expressed by our determined brothers and sisters of green worldview. We may even begin to treasure again the shaman-like older lady who lives down the hall, purple in her worldview, seeing life in magical terms, and praying for magical things. She is no longer a joke to us. And when we get a bad diagnosis, we want her praying for us: not because we share her worldview, but because we feel the gift of her passionate concern and her trust in Power beyond our control and understanding.

As folks move into the turquoise value meme and they open themselves to mystical experience, few will resist the most obvious truths and practical insights of any religion, Christian or otherwise. In the world of turquoise, a new spiritual awakening is not only possible, but very likely.

The church as Holocracy understands this. It creates space even for people who are not theistic, no matter how much they might wish they were able to believe. And it cultivates a place in community for others who may feel powerful impulses of spirituality that simply do not connect well with conventional expressions of church and faith. The church as Holocracy knows that these spaces are not the endgame, but simply places of waiting and possibility—places of sojourn on the journey. They know that to evangelize in such spaces in the old blue ways would be ridiculous and would scatter the people, destroying the community. So it is community for the sake of community, period. And community where we all wait for God's next move.

In our work at Epicenter Group, we have been blessed to work with several faith communities where Holocracy is clearly emerging. Among them: Valley and Mountain Church in Seattle (John Helmiere, convener), Zacc's House in Portland, Oregon (Beth Estock, convener), Imagine in northern Virginia (Dave and Cathy Norman, pastors), and Broken Builders Church in New York City (Paul Moon and Joyce Lee, pastors)

In the latter two examples, two-track systems are in place: a more traditional Christian community existing alongside and in spiritual partnership with a more expansive community of folks. Without Crossroads United Methodist Church in Ashburn, Virginia, the Imagine communities would never have been birthed. The Imagine communities have embraced a couple hundred SBNR kinds of folks on a spiritual journey alongside the more traditional Christians at Crossroads. The same is true in New York City, where Broken Builders Church birthed what it calls the Tutti communities (from the Italian *tutti* meaning "all together")—where they are dancing with God and the neighbors who would otherwise never have walked into their church. As Holocracy becomes more common, we will begin to see such partnerships by the thousands, scattered all across the earth.

In the world of turquoise, Holy Spirit is very real. And Pentecost is always immanent. When a person or a group of persons are emerging into turquoise from yellow, they have touched every color of the spiral in their own personal development. They know the journey and are equipped to become spiritual guides to others on that journey.

They know that eventually, if you are open and growing as a human being, life's journey will carry you through a decidedly love-hate relationship with organized religion to a place where you see again its powerful possibilities. It is at this place where you are open in new and unprecedented ways to the movement and work of the Spirit. And so they trust the Spirit in all things—in every one-on-one relationship, in organizational life, and in their vision of where it is all going.

For the church leaders rising into turquoise, it is not simply that they "refuse to lead a dying church," it is that they are past any notion that the church could die, and so they are also past the fear of such. They know that the church will change, and that it will mature, and that many forms will fall away. They also know that many of their best allies in the building of the next generation of church are not a part of it yet—just neighbors still waiting to be invited to dance.

And best of all, they know in their hearts that Christ is risen—and that as we die with him, so too we all shall rise.

We (Beth and Paul) are watching the emergence of Holocracy in faith communities scattered across the world. It is happening quickly. Most of the time, their turquoise worldview leaders don't even know one another until we or others assist in making the introductions. There is little networking yet. They are emerging too independently, too simultaneously. Their emergence is more related to a Holy Spirit moment in history than to an organized campaign coming out of any ecclesiastical office. As we learn, we are committed to sharing more in the days ahead.

Yes, many of the old school churches are on life support—but do not think for a minute that they are the headline story of twenty-first-century Christianity. There is a new church in town. Rising from the ashes. A gift to coming generations! And it is so beautiful, so elegant, so Spirit-driven. Once your eyes focus and you are *able* to see it, you will send up a hearty prayer of thanks that you *lived* to see it!

POSTREMO

✼

An Altar Call

In Luke 10, Jesus says to the seventy missionaries going out on their spiritual adventure, "The harvest is plentiful, but the laborers are few." Then in John's gospel, "Do you not say, 'Four months and then comes the harvest?' But I tell you, look around you and see how the fields are ripe for harvesting." This theme of a harvest ready now is a critical part of how Jesus read the world around him.

As we noted in the beginning of this book, we are living in a time when the numbers of people responding to conventional Christendom-heritage churches is steadily diminishing. Most of what we consider "effective" churches—Catholic, evangelical, and progressive—have steadily shifted to focus themselves on careful gleaning in a field of disappointing and diminishing return. Think of it as the art of competing for the Christian remnant. Maybe 20 percent of the kids now being raised in Sunday school/children's church will come back to similar churches regularly as adults, based on current trends—maybe a few more, maybe even less. It is easy for us to focus on the art of attracting the prized remnant.

With so many churches trying to survive, and such a puny supply of potential worshipers to work with, it is a survival of the fittest scenario. And if we are unable to shift beyond a moribund institutional paradigm of what church and Christian faith are, then gleaning is about the best we can do.

Or is it possible that we are deeply misreading the moment? Is it possible that there is a bumper crop in the fields that very few Christian leaders are currently discerning? Our best guess is that if Jesus were walking and riding with us in the communities where we live and work and worship, he would see far greater possibilities than gleaning! We cannot imagine Jesus writing off a generation or two, simply because they had moved beyond the worldview of a simpler world, and beyond interest in highly institutionalized religion.

Looking at this reality through the lens of Spiral Dynamics, we discover some pretty good reasons behind what's going on. Even though more people are moving into a secular worldview, and for some an atheistic worldview, we should be careful in assuming that this means a dead-end for Christianity. Because there is no reason to assume that they will simply stop at the subway station called Secular. Millions of people in this century will continue to grow past secularity. As churches emerge that are ready for that growth, some amazing things will happen.

First, as more folks shift into the land of yellow worldview (and beyond), the cartoon-like twentieth-century dualism of fundamentalists yelling back and forth with secularists will begin to seem really silly, really childish, really boring. There is a big century looming before us that moves beyond the current orange-green secularism. In the twenty-first century, increasing numbers of folks will reintegrate faith into their lives, often in ways that would puzzle their great grandparents.

In this rising world of yellow and turquoise worldviews, spirituality becomes so much more than a Sunday hobby or something that can be contained within the programming of any religious organization, or outsourced to religious big business! Faith becomes a very personal and hallowed quest. And, for many, Jesus becomes a mystical and deeply personal friend and guide (reminiscent of eighteenth century pietism, but not bound by the tight walls of blue worldview). Bible students move beyond a fixation on what is literal/historical and what is not, to an exploration of what the ancient texts reveal about the contours of our souls and of ultimate reality. Scriptures will come alive as metaphors containing deep truths and rituals will come to take on new meaning alongside the stories of the communion of saints.

One by one, as our sons and daughters in the land of yellow and turquoise meet Jesus, it will be like fire touching gun powder—with a likely explosion of spiritual energy and discovery reminiscent of the Great Awakenings. But it will also be very different as we see them begin to effectively articulate what it means to be Christian within the complexity of a worldview that few of us have yet experienced. Upon that discovery as foundation, there will inevitably come a rush of Holy Spirit wind upon the earth like unto which none of us have seen in our lifetimes. New institutions, new ways of thinking, new ways of being Christian, new experiences of sacrament, new forms of faith community, and new possibilities for the future of the human race will emerge.

This is the promise of the twenty-first century!

Anyone who assumes that this is a post-Christian century may be utterly dumbfounded by what is around the corner. It is assuredly a post-Christendom century, but the generations coming behind us will also assuredly discover anew what it means to follow the Way of Jesus in their context. If we really believe in Pentecost, how could we expect anything else?

Not every twentieth-century church will disappear in the twenty-first! A few strategic funerals within the church leadership of those old world churches will help them get ready to move with God into the Promised Land. In this book, we have considered several forms of churches—from Cathedral to Dinner Party to Mission Base Camp—that will thrive as the direct legacy of existing spiritually nimble congregations!

But even as a few churches dare to make the journey with God into a place of relevance and fruitful life, most of the existing institutional structures are nearing the end of their effective life. Much of what clergy and denominational leaders are currently invested in is about to evaporate before their very eyes, leaving them in many cases with aging and very expensive buildings and very few human beings. In some cases, they would be wise to begin packing their parachutes—because they will not want to go down with their organizational aircraft—God has called them to so much more than that!

We often tell our church planters, "Show up to whatever you perceive God is doing in your community. Follow that energy." In the decades to come, this would be good coaching for any Christian leader, from church planter to bishop. Indeed, most of the action in the twenty-first century will move beyond the bounds of church membership and institutional programming.

If any existing faith community, church, or denomination is willing and unready to partner with fellow servants of God whose communities *cannot be absorbed* into your current structures—please partner! Such partnership will not save Methodism, Anglicanism, Presbyterianism, and so forth, but it will enable the people within these heritage groups to stay connected to the vital cutting edge of the Spirit's movement upon the earth. It will enable great mentoring, and great sharing of faith traditions and wisdom. There is such great joy and satisfaction in staying connected to fruitfulness.

This kind of opportunity exists for almost every aging church, denomination, faith institution, and leader—for all of us who are the survivors from the last dynasty before Christendom came to a close! Let us bless and mentor young movements and fresh faith expressions!

Move to the edges, if you dare, toward those rising sons and daughters who have long abandoned our houses of worship. Run toward the ones whom the Spirit has captivated in these latest of days—the young artists, and activists, with voices fresh and unorthodox, ready to prophecy. Do not do this selfishly, with the hopes that they will bail out a tired, old church. It is not about us. It is about them. Moreover, it is about transcending all notions of "us and them." To use Paul Moon's metaphor, it is about showing up to dance with God and all the folks God is bringing to her party.

Sometimes the leaders and movements we resource and bless will choose to connect with us organizationally and help keep the spiritual farm alive for another go-round in a new age. Partnerships of old world churches with weird, new world churches—these can be rich.

A few years back, in one of the greenest cities in America (Portland, Maine), the old Chestnut Street Church sold its massive two-hundred-year old building to a developer. The market of church shoppers looking for what Chestnut Street offered had evaporated. About a dozen remnant members began meeting in a nearby synagogue on Sundays. The church released some of its funds for the planting of a new church of simple cells meeting in homes, called New Light. Finally, New Light and Chestnut found a small building from which to base some of their ministries. They named the new building Hope.Gate.Way. and then it went off script. The old people began to show up at the cell groups, and the younger people began to show up at the worship services. There came a day when no one could tell who was Chestnut and who was New Light; and so they just called it all Hope.Gate.Way. We expect to see endless variations on their story in the decades ahead.

In Washington, D.C., the United Methodist Church recently recruited a three-year-old fast-growing nondenominational church (called the Table) to become a ministry partner in serving the metro area. The denomination offered the Table a building in a dynamic neighborhood (where the UMC congregation had closed several years ago), in return for the Table agreeing to affiliate with the denomination and to contribute money to support the work of the denomination (just like a typical UMC congregation). The point is not about raising money for the home office. It's so much more interesting. The Table will work in partnership with the Baltimore Washington Conference of the UMC to plant new faith communities all across the region, to reach and bless young adults in D.C., Maryland, and Virginia. It is possible that a significant multisite movement will emerge in D.C. as collaboration between the UMC and the Table. Now an old denomination gets to play in a kingdom sandbox with hundreds of millennials in America's youngest city.

The UMC will never fully own the Table and never fully control the Table. It is a limited partnership. Therefore, all parties must stay on good behavior. Otherwise, the partnership will end. This kind of measured affiliation is a very promising possibility in all sorts of places in the years ahead. Denominations and congregations that are willing to create such partnerships will love the twenty-first century!

More commonly, however, the young faith community movements will not choose to affiliate organizationally with the old churches. They need some space; they need speed. And they need distance from the old church DNA and bureaucratic inertia that has driven their generation away from institutional religion.

However, even without organizational affiliation, young and old can still dance together! As older churches come to the point where their buildings are too big or too old and/or their crowds too small, they will have opportunities to bless the rising churches by passing along some of their remaining assets. They will have the chance to invest in the rising before they turn to dust.

It all turns to dust, eventually. No expression of church is eternal. All the churches the Apostle Paul planted in Turkey are dust. As we turn this manuscript over to the publisher our two families are about to journey to Ephesus and walk the ruins. We will see ruins of the basilica that was eventually inhabited by the amazing church Paul founded there. Only ruins. And dust. No church is left there. But we are their legacy! God created a world where new life is ever arising from the residue of past life.

On the one hand, to witness the declining institutional church trying so desperately to save its organizational life is both embarrassing and deeply frustrating. On the other hand, to witness the same church sighing a collective "what the hell" and giving up on people under age sixty is absolutely maddening! And then watching them spend down their last resources entirely on themselves is tragic.

We pray for more churches that would discover the joy of partnering with the weird new movements and leaders that arise from green, yellow, and turquoise awareness, much like grandmothers launching their progeny into life with love. Grandmothers look at their grandchildren, mystified by the strange ideas and practices, the technological prowess, and the amazing capacities for thriving in a world of complexity. Even though grandkids can seem like space aliens, grandmothers hold them close and love them tenderly. They pray for them daily. They bless the grandkids with all that is within them—even though they have absolutely nothing personal to gain from this ultimately, except joy. Those same grandmothers often seek to leave resources for the grandchildren so that the future might truly be collaboration, in which the gifts of multiple generations are comingled together, even as the stage clearly and fully passes from the old to the young.

There is really nothing weird at all about that.

NOTES

1. Ed Stetzer, Micah Fries, and Daniel Im, "The State of Church Planting in the U.S.," LifeWay Research and NewChurches.com, 2015, https://newchurches.com/wp-content/uploads/2015/09/NewChurches.com-State-of-Church-Planting-in-the-U.S.-2015-Report.pdf. Data is based upon survey-gathered data from 843 church planters across seventeen different denominational and church-planting network organizations.

2. One well-known faith development theory was offered by James Fowler in his 1981 book *Stages of Faith* (New York: Harper and Row). Fowler sought to develop the idea of a developmental process in "human faith" much like Jean Piaget's theory of cognitive development and Lawrence Kohlberg's stages of moral development. We recommend Ken Wilber's book *Integral Spirituality: A Startling New Role for Religion in the Modern and Postmodern World* (Boulder, CO: Shambala, 2007), in which he outlines integral theory and the church's role in our healthy evolutionary development.

3. Holocracy (also spelled holacracy) is a new way of running an organization that removes power from a management hierarchy and distributes it across clear roles, which can then be executed autonomously, without a micromanaging boss (http://www.holacracy.org/how-it-works/). An excellent book about this emerging field is Frederick Laloux and Ken Wilder, *Reinventing Organizations* (Brussels: Nelson Parker, 2014).

4. Bridges borrows this concept from anthropologist Arnold van Gennep, who talked about change in human life as having three phases: (1) endings, (2) neutral space, and (3) new beginnings. Bridges' classic work *Managing Transitions* (Jackson, TN: Da Capo Books, 2009) unpacks these ideas in detail.

5. From Lovett Weems's *Focus: The Real Challenges That Face the United Methodist Church*, Adaptive Leadership Series (Nashville: Abingdon Press, 2012).

6. Joe Freisen, "Faith Groups' Capacity for Sponsoring Refugees Is Collapsing," *The Globe and Mail*, Sept. 21, 2015, p. 3.

7. In chapter 17, we will see that the Community Center church remains one of the models of the future—but it is much more than the late Christendom idea of a venue for educating and entertaining church members and their kids.

8. Clay Shirky, "Institution vs. collaboration," TED talk filmed July 2005, http://www.ted.com/talks/clay_shirky_on_institutions_versus_collaboration?.

9. Robert King, "Death and Resurrection of an urban church," Faith and Leadership, https://www.faithandleadership.com/death-and-resurrection-urban-church.

10. "Edict of Toleration by Galerius," https://en.wikipedia.org/wiki/Edict_of _Toleration_by_Galerius.

11. "Edict of Milan," https://en.wikipedia.org/wiki/Edict_of_Milan.

12. Brian J. Walsh and Sylvia C. Keesmaat, *Colossians Remixed: Subverting the Empire* (Westmont, IL: IVP Academic, 2004), 29.

13. Ibid., 30.

14. Howard Thurman, quoted in Gil Bailie's *Violence Unveiled* (New York: Crossroad, 1996), xv.

15. This information about the thousand-person cap per church was mentioned to Paul Nixon by Chinese church leaders more than once in his visit to China in spring 2011.

16. Open Space Technology (OST) is a simple way to run productive meetings, for five to two thousand or more people, and a powerful approach to leadership in any kind of organization, in everyday practice and turbulent change (see http ://openspaceworld.org/wp2/).

17. Heinrich Bolleter, "The Risen Christ Behind Closed Doors," a sermon preached at Crescent Hill UMC, Louisville, Kentucky, on May 10, 1992.

18. The so-called "Francis Effect" is an idea drawn from anecdotal observations of a slight uptick in attendance at Mass in countries where the pope is very popular. As of this writing, it is still hard to document whether Francis is significantly impacting people's openness to the Catholic Church.

19. The Barna Group and Cornerstone Knowledge Network, "Making Space for Millennials: A Blueprint for Your Culture, Ministry, Leadership and Facilities," report, 2014, 11.

20. MissionInsight, LLC, "The Quadrennium Project 2012," white paper, fall 2012, http://missioninsite.com/wp-content/uploads/2013/01/Quadrennium White Paper.pdf; Pew Research Center, "U.S. Public Becoming Less Religious," November 3, 2015, http://www.pewforum.org/2015/11/03/u-s-public-becoming -less-religious/.

21. Barna Group, "10 Facts about America's Churches," Articles in Culture and Media, December 10, 2014, https://www.barna.org/barna-update/culture/698 -10-facts-about-america-s-churchless#.VQnp6imy6go.

22. In the green Spiral Dynamics worldview where personal truth comes in the form of experience, ritual becomes highly important. I may not believe what you

believe, but invite me into a centuries-old ritual and I can experience the holy for myself and make up my own mind.

23. Timothy George, *Guaranteed Pure: Moody Bible Institute, Business and the Making of American Evangelicalism* (Chapel Hill: University of North Carolina Press, 2015).

24. Interesting to note that in 1544 the Council of Trent declared as official Catholic doctrine that original sin is spread by semen.

25. Tony Jones, *Did God Kill Jesus?* (New York: HarperOne, 2015), 119.

26. Ibid., 125.

27. Melissa Binder, "Yes, Portland is America's most religiously unaffiliated metro. But who exactly are the 'nones'?" Oregon Live, March 18, 2015, "http://www.oregonlive.com/faith/2015/03/portland_unaffiliated.html#incart_most -readnews.

28. *Imago Dei* is Latin for "made in God's image." It points to a foundational concept in Christianity, Judaism, and some branches of Islam asserting that human beings possess special qualities through which we can see aspects of God's nature.

29. Cynthia Bourgeaul, *The Wisdom Jesus* (Boston: Shambhala, 2008), 14.

30. Ibid., 21.

31. Ibid., 73.

32. Attributed to Chardin in Robert J. Gurey, *The Joy of Kindness* (New York: Crossroad, 1993).

33. Lectio divina is a traditional Benedictine practice of reading scripture that is intended to promote communion with God. It has four separate steps: read; meditate; pray; contemplate.

34. Frederick Schleiermacher, *Addresses on Religion*, 1799. Quoted in Elie Kedourie, *Nationalism* 4th ed., (Oxford, UK: Blackwell, 1993), 18.

35. Joni Mitchell, "Woodstock," *Message to Love: The Isle of Wight Festival*, 1970, ©Siquomb Publishing; lyrics at http://jonimitchell.com/music/song.cfm?id=75.

36. M. G. Seigler, "Eric Schmidt: Every 2 Days We Create As Much Information A We Did Up to 2003," Tech Crunch Network, August 4, 2010, http://techcrunch .com/2010/08/04/scmidt-data/.

37. Thad McIlroy, "The Future of Newspapers," The Future of Publishing, blog, http://thefutureofpublishing.com/industries/the-future-of-newspapers/.

38. One unexpected, perhaps unintended, consequence of the broadcast model is the tendency for more people to be shaped and formed as consumers of a brand of Christianity rather than disciples of Christ, especially if we use small group formation as a means toward mass indoctrination or for herding people for the large group gathering. If we are not thoughtful, we can end up playing church instead of being the church.

39. Paul: The savviest broadcast model church that I have worked with in the last decade has grown phenomenally in just a few years from one hundred people to a megachurch with multiple locations. Everyone is wowed by them. But these guys are smart: they also lead their denomination in the development of their online campus—which is still largely broadcast, but is opening the door to an increasingly interactive web world at the heart of their faith community.

40. "Your Weekly Address," the White House Briefing Room site, https://www.whitehouse.gov/briefing-room/weekly-address.

41. Catherine Taibi, "Here's How the Way We Read Newspapers Has Changed," Huffington Post, May 21, 2014, http://www.huffingtonpost.com/2014/05/21/newspaper-evolution-change-infographic-digital-twitter-online_n_5367077.html.

42. Vine is an app of looping six-second videos that launched in 2013, challenging the primacy of YouTube as the premier media platform. Imagine using this platform as a way to invite millennials to experience Christian rituals.

43. Found in Barbara Brown Taylor, *Gospel Medicine* (Plymouth, UK: Rowman & Littlefield, 1995), 153.

44. Newspaper editor John O'Sullivan coined the term "manifest destiny" in 1845, a term that pointed to the special virtues of the American people and their institutions, plus America's irresistible mission and destiny to redeem and remake the Western Hemisphere in the image of U.S. culture. For further reading, we recommend Robert J. Miller, *Native America, Discovered and Conquered: Thomas Jefferson, Lewis & Clark, and Manifest Destiny* (Westport, CT: Praeger, 2006).

45. The Church Growth movement was an intensely utilitarian emphasis on finding theology and method that would yield more church participants. Highly influenced by missiologist Donald McGavran, this school of thought influenced a generation of Protestant pastors who sought to turn the tide of church decline, specifically by a hyperfocus on strategies and tactics for growing local congregations. The explosion of the megachurches and multisites came as a partial result, even as the overall trajectory of Christian participation continued to decline.

46. The Brightmoor Aldersgate Free Store is a place where neighborhood residents can "shop" for basic household items, without paying money. The store's inventory is collected from area churches and donors, much like goods are collected for a rummage sale, but there is no cash box. Within certain limitations per customer, the merchandise is distributed freely to people who are in need.

47. Tom Rath and Barry Conchie, in their book *Strengths Based Leadership* (Gallup Press, 2013), report on what followers are looking for in leaders. From their Gallup survey they discovered that the four basic needs of followers are trust, compassion, stability, and hope. When leaders meet these basic needs, people naturally follow. Much of our emphasis on incarnational leadership can also be viewed through the

lens of emotional and social intelligences. The capacities for self-awareness, self-management, social awareness, and relationship management are crucial for the healthy unfolding of faith communities in this century. We recommend reading *Primal Leadership* (Cambridge, MA: Harvard Business Review Press, 2004) by Daniel Goleman, Richard Boyatz, and Annie Mckee for a more in-depth study of the qualities of incarnational leaders.

48. By late century and beyond, the human genome itself may be changing via technological advances and genetic engineering. This poses a significant wild card as to what faith will look like in the more distant future. The eventual demise of homo sapiens could be more a matter of our genetic manipulation/creation of the next race of humans rather than a violent ending in a nuclear or ecological catastrophe. We may also begin to see a blurring of the lines between human and human-manufactured intelligence. For these reasons, the possibilities of weird church a century from now could run well off the page. For an in-depth study of the possibilities, we recommend Yuval Noah Harari's *Sapiens: A Brief History of Humankind* (New York; Harper Collins, 2015).

49. Lectio divina is a prayer-filled way of reading scripture that asks three questions: 1. What word or phrase speaks to me? 2. How does this story relate to my story? 3. How am I being called to grow as a result of hearing this story?

50. The Schweiberts' inspiring memoir published through Grief Watch is called *Resistance and Redirection: Our First Forty Years* (Portland, OR: Grief Watch, 2015).

51. Based on the experience of Simple Church, Grafton, Massachusetts, Zach Kerzee, pastor.

52. Mark Oppenheimer, "Young Methodists Plant Churches with Environmental Gospel," *New York Times*, September 4, 2015.

53. Please note here the overlap with the Community Center model of church—which may or may not involve a small enterprise. Conversely note that small enterprise can happen without the church even having a public location.

54. For more about this model, see Paul's very first book, *Fling Open the Doors: Giving the Church Away to the Community* (Nashville: Abingdon, 2002).

55. Jerry Herships, *Last Call: From Serving Drinks to Serving Jesus* (Louisville: Westminster-John Knox Press, 2015).

56. We are using the term "cathedral" in a broad manner, beyond simply the church where the bishop is stationed, to consider all kinds of worship facilities with soaring and inspirational space.